# SWINDON GWR REMINISCENCES

# SWINDON

**GWR**

# REMINISCENCES

Eric R. Mountford

BRADFORD BARTON

ISBN 0 85153 438 4
copyright © Eric R. Mountford
set and printed by CTP Ltd for Top Link Ltd
for the publishers
D. BRADFORD BARTON LTD
Trethellan House · Truro · England

BD0195

# CONTENTS

'The G.W.R. works at Swindon in the 1920s and early 1930s was at its zenith. Alone amongst the major railways of this country, the Great Western had been unruffled, even strengthened, by the extensive amalgamations of 1922/23 and Swindon was the centre for the design, construction and maintenance of the company's locomotives and rolling stock.

The 1925 and 1926 locomotive exchanges with the much larger L.N.E.R. and L.M.S. groups had proved the superiority of the G.W.R. engines in each case and being followed in 1927 by the triumphant visit of 6000 *King George V* to U.S.A. it heralded a period when the name of Swindon was on the lips of everyone connected with, or interested in, railway locomotives. In short, the G.W.R. was supreme and Swindon was the showplace of that supremacy.

Swindon itself was virtually a one hundred per cent railway town. Of its population of around 55,000, well over a quarter were directly employed by the G.W.R., whilst the remainder consisted of the families of those employees plus the tradesmen and others who catered for their everyday needs.

It was at that period and in that atmosphere that the author grew up – through his schooldays and followed by an apprenticeship at the works from 1933 onwards. In these pages he relates his memories in the railway town, through his boyhood days as a locomotive enthusiast and finally his apprenticeship. It is intended to be a human rather than a purely technical story, full of interest about the engines, the works and the town. It is tinged with humour when relating some of the day-to-day events and also recalls many of the men the author worked with and for. There is also coverage of the relationship of the G.W.R. with the town and the immense benefits that their employees received from the railway. It is a story that should commend itself to one interested in the G.W.R. and its locomotives, or in the history of the town of Swindon.

# 1

## *Memories, 1923–1937*

LOOKING BACK WELL over half a century, one has to separate railway recollections from what could possibly be fantasy based on photographs of the period, coupled with the historical records now available. In my case railway recollections of the years 1923 and 1924 are few and far between, but from 1925 onwards my enthusiasm for G.W.R. locomotives was so great that the railway scene at Swindon in those days stands out as sharply today as if it were only yesterday. Although my railway memories are vague before that date, it is strange that I can clearly recollect my first day at Infant School in September 1920, when I was three years of age. A small wooden-edged slate was put on the desk in front of me, and a layer of sand poured on it. The teacher chalked letters and numbers on the blackboard, which I attempted to copy in the sand with my index finger – a cheap and useful method of teaching, as mistakes could so easily be rectified.

Having been born in Swindon and living in Jolliffe Street, only a stone's throw from the huge A Erecting Shop – the finest locomotive workshop in the world in those days – engines soon got into my blood. However, I have no recollection of any individual engine until 1923, when I was taken to the top of nearby Park Lane to watch the G.W. Pacific *The Great Bear* pass over the railway bridge with its train. Whilst I can only remember the huge engine vaguely, I do recall that the nights were drawing in fast, hence it must have been in the Autumn, only a few weeks before the engine was taken out of traffic and a few parts used to build the Castle class *Viscount Churchill*. At the time, however, Swindon was still talking about the massive Pacific with almost reverence despite, as I found out much later, its having been something of a white elephant.

The following year Swindon was graced by a Royal Visit when King George V and Queen Mary toured the railway workshops on 28 April 1924. We youngsters were taken to near the Town Hall, where we waved miniature Union Jacks as the royal party passed. The next day someone told me that the King had driven *Windsor Castle* from the sidings outside the A Shop to the station and I recall wondering, rather ungraciously, how the King had learned to drive a railway engine so quickly . . .

A few weeks later, probably Whitsun 1924, we went on a Sunday School outing to Marlborough Forest. We had to walk up the hill to the former Midland & South Western Junction Railway station, always known as Old Town station to Swindonians, to catch the train which I clearly remember was headed by a 4–4–0 gleaming in the red livery of that company. The carriages were also of much the same colour; although I did not realise it at the time, this was the only complete train in pre-group livery that I should ever remember seeing. Although the G.W.R. had taken over the M.S.W.J. a few months previously, changes did not take place overnight, and Old Town station was still a peaceful backwater, far removed from the bustling G.W. workshops, sidings and station below.

Railway engines were still far from being my only interest. It was about that time that my brother Cyril, three years older than myself, had a tiny crystal wireless set, which he kept in an outside shed. To my tender years it all seemed amazing, as the only home entertainment we were used to was singing around the piano. The set was incredibly simple. All I recall was a small wooden base on which the crystal was mounted. On one side was a tiny fulcrum, on which a small rod with a short length of wire at the end could be controlled. I suppose there was also some flex and a pair of earphones. By turning the small rod, the wire scratched over the surface of the crystal and eventually you hit on a spot where sounds could be heard. The first I picked up was a lady singing, and no doubt in London it sounded fine, but from that tiny crystal set in the back yard shed it sounded shrill and distorted.

The year 1925 saw the beginning of a lifetime of enthusiasm for the steam engine, particularly those belonging to the G.W.R. By that time I could differentiate between the principal classes, and realised that a large number of the engines on the sidings around the loco works did not originate at Swindon. Throughout the year there were a considerable number of tank engines of various shapes and sizes that had uncovered safety valves showing above the boilers. That was a horror as far as Swindon works was concerned, akin to a lady showing her legs – and that was not done either in those days. I knew that these tank engines had been acquired from the railways of South Wales, taken over by G.W.R. and I assumed, in true Swindon manner of the period, that they had been sent in to be put right, not merely repaired.

Initially all the constituent engines were called Cambrians by the youthful enthusiasts of the day, probably because the first batches of engines sent to Swindon followng the 1922 amalgamations were mainly from the Cambrian Railways, and the name had stuck. By 1925 I realised that several other railways besides the Cambrian had been involved, and the engines were then often referred to as Taff Vales as an alternative, probably because that was the largest and best known of the South Wales companies involved. It was a year or two later before I knew the names of all the railway companies involved, and could normally distinguish between the engines of each. Although it may now seem strange, with the avalanche of books available on the subject, in those days there was little literature about railways, and what there was did not deal with such remote subjects as the locomotive stocks of minor railways. In much later years I found out that an occasional magazine had dealt with some of the engines, but there were no ready references available, and with so little pocket money available in any case, we were completely in the dark as to details of the engines we saw, merely recording their numbers.

The other 'foreign' engines I remember, in the latter half of 1925, were a large number of gaunt black tender engines with long domed boilers, which were congregated on the sidings around the works. These engines had the initials R.O.D. in large white letters on the sides of the tenders, followed by the engine number in similar style. We knew these were war surplus engines and that a number had been stored on sidings at an ordnance depot at Stratton, a mile or so north east of Swindon. We youngsters, in true Great Western style, had utter disdain for large engines with domes, and considered that only shunting or very old goods engines should suffer such an indignity.

However, in 1925, the whole town was more concerned with the exploits of the Castle class. Such engines as the R.O.D.'s, or those from South Wales, were easily forgotten as the fame of the Castles grew rapidly. At the 1924 British Empire Exhibition, held at Wembley, the G.W.R. had put on display *Caerphilly Castle*. It was said in the town that a notice placed alongside the engine stated that it was the most powerful in the British Isles, and that the L.N.E.R., who had their larger Pacific *Flying Scotsman* on display nearby, doubted the claim and had challenged the G.W.R. to tests between the engines to prove the statement. The resultant locomotive trials, ending in May 1925, when 4079 *Pendennis Castle* worked on the L.N.E.R. and that company's Pacific 4474 worked on the G.W.R., fired the imagination of the Wiltshire railway town. When the results were made public, everyone in the town was jubilant that the Swindon-built engine had come out well on top, and were confident that the Castles were the best passenger engines on British metals at the time. The following month the engine that the King had driven the previous year, *Windsor Castle*, was selected to take part in the Stockton & Darlington Railway Centenary Celebrations, and this was taken as further evidence of the high esteem in which the Castle class was held beyond the boundaries of the G.W.

Later that year I had to suffer my first railway disappointment. The victorious *Pendennis Castle*, fresh from its triumphs in the locomotive exchanges had, not surprisingly, been chosen to represent the G.W.R. at the 1925 Wembley Exhibition. We were told that parties of Swindon schoolchildren were to be taken to Wembley on 4 September and naturally I was thrilled at the prospect of going. Unfortunately it turned out that there was an age limit for attendance, and at eight I did not qualify. My brother, then eleven years of age, was allowed to go and I had to be content to listen to his views on the exhibition and on 4079. As he was only mildly interested in engines, I did feel somewhat cheated.

In those early school days, my regular haunt for watching trains, and shunting activity around the loco works, was a works boundary fence known as The Boards. This still stands at the back of Dean Street at the western end of town, running parallel to both the main line and the adjacent A Erecting Shop. The eastern end of the boundary was a red brick wall, a little over six feet high, whilst the remainder – about twice the length of the wall, was a timber fence of much the same height. Whilst the brick wall was individually known as The Wall, the whole boundary was normally just called The Boards. The main line was some seventy yards from the fence, whilst beyond the sidings the A Shop would be about 120 yards distant.

It was far from an ideal spot to watch train movements, but it was very close to Jolliffe Street and my school, Westcott. Between The Boards and the main line there were three large timber drying sheds, and in the yard between these were stacked huge piles of timber for seasoning. There were only four or five places along the whole length which gave a view of the main line, and these were only about twelve to fifteen feet wide, being pathways intended for vehicle movement. The most popular spot was where the timber fence adjoined the wall and it was there, either perched on top of a fence support post, or sitting in more comfort at the end of the wall, that I spent a great deal of my off-school hours.

Another spot that had to be visited daily was towards the eastern end of the wall, which gave a reasonable view of the turntable area where engines were stabled after their trial runs. To get there one had to walk along the top of the wall, on which the capping bricks were but a few inches wide. A third and most popular spot was almost at the western end of the wooden fence, from where the huge traverser table doors of A Shop could be seen, as it was on that table that most of the larger engines were taken into shop for repair, or moved out after repair, as well as where all new construction first saw light of day. At all three places, trains on the main line could be seen as well. One soon learned to read the number on an engine in the twinkling of an eye, as that was about all the time one had when a fast train passed one of the twelve foot gaps mentioned.

Despite being a town with intense passion for everything Great Western, there were very few long-lasting railway enthusiasts. Quite a number of schoolboys were engine spotters for a while, but the initial interest usually waned in the face of other hobbies, or by being constantly told by our elders that we would very soon lose interest when 'we started inside'. The vast majority of the boys left school at fourteen and started work in the railway factory, and the whole town referred to anyone who worked in any part of the works as being 'inside'. Swindon was such a one-industry town that you never asked anyone where they worked, merely which (work) shop they worked in.

Returning to the small number of enthusiasts, one of the principal reasons was the lack of information readily available, coupled with little incentive for the hobby, there being no clubs or societies catering for the junior enthusiast, as there are today. With so little information to go on, one had to compile lists of engines as best one could from personal observation. True the G.W.R. issued their booklet 'Names, Numbers, Types and Classes' once a year, but, apart from being months out of date by the time it was available, the detail for other than named engines was scanty or, in numerous cases, non-existent. There were, for example, no details for about ninety per cent of the 0-6-0 saddle and pannier tanks which were to be seen daily, nor for the numerous double-framed 0–6–0 goods engines. The small 0–4–2 tank engines that could be seen everywhere on station shunting duties did not merit a mention, and the 2–4–0Ts and 0–4–0Ts did not appear to exist either. Even in the named engine section, some, such as 2194 *Kidwelly* and 2195 *Cwm Mawr*, which had been at the works under repair for a considerable time, did not warrant a mention either and one wondered how many other similar non-standard named engines there were.

Hence you made up your own lists and tried to achieve some sort of accuracy, made all the more difficult by the renumbering scheme for absorbed engines. These were given blank numbers between Nos. 1 and 2199 in the G.W.R. series, which resulted in seeing a Taff Vale 0–6–2T numbered in the midst of a batch of standard G.W. 0–4–2Ts, or the French engines Nos. 102 to 104 in the middle of a large batch of old Rhymney double-framed 0–6–2STs. It was all rather confusing without any guidance but, to me at least, that was part of the thrill of being an enthusiast in those far-off days – you did not know what would turn up next, or what number it would be carrying. Nowadays, some of the pleasure of the hobby is missing by knowing everything that is going to happen well in advance.

My main enthusiast friend in those days was Hadyn Robinson, whose father kept a draper's shop in Curtis Street. During quiet spells at The Boards, Hadyn and I memorised the engine names and numbers as given in the G.W.R. booklet, testing each other until we could recite each class without error. Having seen him again recently, fifty five years later, we found that we still remembered most of them. Fortunately those early days were before the monotony of lengthy class names, such as the Halls and Castles, the number of the latter class then in existence not having reached the monotonous level. We memorised them up to 5012 *Berry Pomeroy Castle*, but after that gave it up as a bad job. The earlier engines seemed to have such delightful names – *Merlin*, *Tre Pol and Pen*, *Brasenose*, *One and All*, *Kekewich* and *Calceolaria*. Even the 29xx class 4–6–0s had some stirring names – *Lady Disdain*, *Rob Roy*, *Lalla Rookh* and *Robins Bolitho*. Whoever chose the names in the late Victorian and Edwardian eras must have been inspired, but whoever decided on an endless succession of Halls, Castes and Granges certainly got the thumbs-down from most enthusiasts of the 1930s.

In the 1920s we, naturally, called the named engines Namers, apart from those carrying the oval combined name and number plates on the cabsides, which we termed Ringers. Engines without names, particularly tender engines, were known as Nonkers. Smaller tank engines, particularly 0–4–2T and 0–6–0PT or ST, were usually called Bunks, no distinction being made whether it was on shunting or local branch passenger work. Thus the ancient double-framed pannier or saddle tank that shunted the A Shop yard was known as the A Shop Bunk, whilst the engine that worked the Swindon Junction to Swindon Town shuttle service was referred to as the Old Town Bunk.

Returning to The Boards, I would estimate that, between 1925 and 1929, I saw the majority of the existing G.W.R. locomotive fleet, both named and unnamed, from my perch on the fence. During 1925 I remember some of the new Castle class emerging from A Shop for the first time, particularly 4089–4092 viz *Donnington, Dorchester, Dudley* and *Dunraven Castle*. That was even before their tenders had been attached. As they appeared only a few weeks after the trials carried out between *Pendennis Castle* and the L.N.E.R. Pacific, we youngsters regarded the Castle class with about the same kind of admiration that those of similar age look on space craft today. Apart from the R.O.D. and Welsh engines mentioned earlier, we also saw, in 1925, an endless succession of the new 56xx class 0–6–2Ts which had been built at the works for use in the South Wales coalfield.

The year 1926 followed a similar pattern in many respects, more new Castle class, and more of the 0–6–Ts for South Wales. However the R.O.D.s caused considerable interest that year. They were taken into the A Shop in fairly large numbers and the thirty that were selected to be rebuilt and retained, returned to traffic, freshly painted G.W. green, with covers over the safety valves and 'Great Western' on the tender sides. As such, we reluctantly accepted them as 'proper' G.W. engines. The other fifty were touched up, painted black or just rubbed down with paraffin rags, and sent back to work until needing heavy repair. We knew that these were destined for the scrap heap when that day arrived and, sure enough, within two or three years they were back for cutting up. The practice of painting engines black when due for scrapping at the next heavy repair was extended to numerous G.W.R. engines a year or two later, particularly to shunting engines, and indicated to us which were due for the chop.

Another event which stands out in my mind was the General Strike in May 1926. For a few days the giant works were silent, no shunters fussing around the yards and, initially at least, no trains on the main line. The uncanny silence of the workshops made it seem like a succession of Sundays for those few days, even more so as there were normally quite a number of main line train movements on Sundays.

Soon after the strike was over, and during my school summer holidays, I was sitting at the west end of the Boards on a sunny July morning, when I saw what appeared to be a new 0–6–2T slowly emerge from the A shop on the traversing table. I could see that it was not a 56xx class, despite the copper-capped chimney and polished brass safety valve cover. Besides being somewhat smaller, there was something different, and it soon dawned on me that the top of the tank was straight for the whole length, and not sloping at the front end as on the 56xx class. It carried the number 34, the plate having the tell-tale initials G.W.R. between the top ring and the number which, even by 1926, clearly indicated that the engine was from a constituent/absorbed company. No. 34 was, of course, one of the former Rhymney Railway side tanks which Swindon decided to experiment with by rebuilding with a Standard No. 2 tapered boiler.

The locomotive engineers at Swindon were so impressed with both the design and maintenance of modern Rhymney boilers that No. 34 was the only Rhymney engine rebuilt thus at Swindon, although several were later done at Caerphilly. Even so, quite a number retained original Rhymney boilers until scrapped in the 1950s. No. 34, as rebuilt in 1926, was beautifully turned out in G.W. green, but by the time I next saw it, a few years afterwards, it had lost the copper-capped chimney for a cast-iron tapered one, and the polished valve cover had been painted over.

Two other constituent engines also stand out in my memory from that 1926 Summer. These were 0–6–0 saddle tanks Nos. 674 and 676 which had been taken over from the Alexandra (Newport and South Wales) Docks and Railway, although I hasten to add that I was un-aware of that at the time. Both had been around the works, in pieces, for a long time waiting their turn for a place in the workshop. No. 676 had been there since November 1922, and 674 from January 1923. When they came out of shop together in May 1926 they had not been altered externally in any drastic way, although they received tall G.W. parallel chimneys, and had their bunkers rebuilt to Swindon style. However what did look odd were the safety valve covers fitted. As received at Swindon, the engines had a small dome, with cover, and the safety valves exposed on the top. Hence as all valve stems had to be covered, a special valve cover was designed to go on top of the dome cover. To us, used to seeing separate dome and safety valve covers, the combination on those two Welsh engines looked very odd. They were painted green and shunted around the yards for a few days before being sent back to Newport. A short time later I saw some former Port Talbot Railway engines, also 0–6–0 saddle tanks, which had similarly been fitted with the same type of combined dome and safety valve cover. Later still I found out that these had been fitted at Swindon before the 1922 amalgamations, at a time when the G.W.R. were working the Port Talbot line by arrangement, but the covers fitted to Nos. 674 and 676 were the first I actually saw.

I suppose of all my recollections of 1926 the one which overshadowed all others was my first sighting of one of the French engines, No 102 *La France*, in October. This was the one and only time I saw it. The tender had been removed and it was standing towards the west end of the A Shop, and not on one of the two reception sidings reserved for engines waiting attention in the shop. It was in a fairly dirty condition, but complete with name and number plates, the name being on a small straight plate on the cabside below the number plate. I somehow realised that No. 102 had been withdrawn for scrapping, and I assumed it was waiting entry to the A Shop to have its boiler taken out, before being pushed further westwards to the scrap yard.

Shortly afterwards, I saw No. 103 *President* pass The Boards on a passenger train, but this was also taken out of service early the following year, leaving the third engine, No. 104 *Alliance*, to carry on as the sole survivor until August 1928. During 1927 and 1928 I saw *Alliance* several times on up passenger trains. Although shedded at Oxford, it worked through to Bristol on occasions, and it was on the return workings that I saw it. When a French engine was approaching on a train, you knew long before you could see it – a sound somewhat similar to that of the steam rail cars, but smoother and far less noisy. Nos. 103 and 104 did not look quite so 'foreign' as did 102, probably because they carried standard copper-capped chimneys, polished brass safety valve covers and standard type nameplates over the rear driving wheel splashers, whereas No. 102 had a cast-iron tapered chimney as well as the non-standard nameplate. Although I did not realise the signficance of the French engines at the time, I later realised I had been fortunate to see them as they were part of the Great Western scene of the period before intense standardisation set in.

Despite the numerous happenings that I witnessed from The Boards in 1927, one will always stand out in my memory. It was a hot sunny day in June, late morning, and I was at the west end opposite the traverser doors. After a while I could see the table coming up the shop and in the dark shadows inside the shop could just be made out a large engine on the table. As it emerged into the sunshine I could see it was painted grey and lined out, looking like a longer, but lower, version of a Castle. I quickly made out the name and number, 6000 *King George V*; it was then that I realised that I was witnessing the birth of a brand new class of G.W.R. express passenger engines. It was quickly pulled away by the A Shop pilot to near the east end of the shop where a new type of tender, also painted grey, was attached. The pair were then pushed down to the south-west corner, near the Weighbridge House, where official photographs were taken. From the records it would appear that the date was Friday 24 June, an important date to me as I must have been the first enthusiast to see the completed engine, witnessing it actually emerging from the shop. No doubt others saw it under construction, but that day I saw the finished locomotive, and to an unashamed G.W. enthusiast, it was a sheer joy to behold.

As previously mentioned, one of the delights of being a young enthusiast in those days was the lack of knowledge of what was happening in the locomotive world until after it was a *fait accompli*. As far as the 'King' was concerned I had not even heard a whisper that it was under construction – and I only lived a quarter of a mile from the Works. I have often wondered why; perhaps it was because I came from a family of coach body builders, who had little knowledge of what was going on at the locomotive side of the works. That theory was rapidly discounted as the fathers of several of my school friends worked in the loco. works, and they did not know either. Whatever the reason, I certainly heard nothing about the construction of the new class until I actually saw 6000 emerge into the sunshine late that June morning.

A brief word on official locomotive photographs of that period. I consider that, by painting engines grey, and also cutting out any signs of the background, dull and lifeless photographs resulted. They also gave one a feeling of frustration – that there was something, in fact a great deal, missing in the picture. What I did not realise at the time was the amount of time, expense and work that was put in to produce these photographs. First the engine itself had to be painted grey, and go through the routine of being taken out of the shops, having a tender attached, and being taken to the standard location for such photographs. When the works photographer had removed the hood for the last time, the reverse procedure had to take place, with both engine and tender going back into the shops for repainting. As there was no separate paint shop at Swindon, it had to occupy valuable pit space whilst the painting took place.

The photographer had a more tedious job. When he had completed his glass plate negative, he had to carefully paint out all traces of the background. This may been comparatively easy if the subject had been a straightforward object, but think of the difficulties connected with blocking-out the background of a railway engine, carefully painting out around the chimney, whistles and cab, handrails, between the spokes of the wheels, etc. Just think of painting around the brake and water scoop handles on the tender, and between the rods of the brake gear below. Fortunately the practice ceased a year or two later, probably with the introduction of film for photographs in place of the old glass plates but, whatever the reason, I for one was very pleased – and so, one imagines, was the photographic staff.

Another engine I particularly remember seeing at the works in 1927 was 'Metro' tank 3593. This had been rebuilt as a 2–4–2T many years earlier, and as such the rear end with its high-roofed cab looked out of proportion. No. 3593 had been fitted with larger and taller side tanks that blotted out of sight most of the boiler. It also had a much larger bunker than the other Metro tanks, in fact the cab and bunker seemed quite big enough for a much larger design. Apart from the engine itself, what was most unusual was that it came down from the Works reception sidings, later known as the Triangle area, on a Saturday afternoon in November. Although Saturday mornings were part of the normal working week in those days, the works were closed from noon on Saturday until eight o'clock on Monday morning. Overtime was not the order of the day at pre-war Swindon Works, and despite the countless loco movements during the working week all went quiet over the weekend. No. 3593 was propelled to the A Shop yard by the East End pilot, which had to do its own shunting in the A Shop area to place it on the right siding. I cannot recollect another incidence of either loco movements in the loco yard on a Saturday afternoon, or of the East End pilot shunting in the A Shop yard. Normally the two locomotive pilots had their own well-defined duties, and were not even stabled together at the weekend. I never learned the reason for the urgency to get 3593 to the A Shop area, as it ended up in the scrap yard a few days afterwards.

# 2

## The Dump, 1925–1927

TURNING SOUTHWARDS from the end of Dean Street was a footpath through some allotments which led to a recreation ground known as the West End Rec. This consisted of two quite large playing areas divided by a small stream, the River Ray. Along the south side of the rec. ran the Wootton Bassett Road, whilst at the west end was a railway embankment for the main line to Bristol or South Wales. Beyond the main line and its accompanying Up Relief line, there was a string of eighteen sidings known from that day to this as The Dump, despite the sidings mentioned having been taken up about 1977. The Dump was always a fascinating place, but never so much as in the mid and late 1920s.

The sidings were full of withdrawn or stored engines, carriages and wagons, mainly from the railways that the G.W.R. had taken over in 1922/23, although a few standard G.W. engines were stored there in 1925/26 due to the recession. There was also other rolling stock on the sidings such as old mineral brake vans, horse boxes and travelling hand cranes, in fact anything on wheels that the works wanted to forget for a while, and which was mostly destined for the scrap heap anyway.

I never learned the history of the sidings, but probably they were only laid down a few years earlier, perhaps during the First World War. In the 1920s engines being sent to The Dump often had the word *Military* chalked on the cab side, although sometimes the word *Field* was used as an alternative. Many latter-day enthusiasts assumed that the rows of broad gauge engines awaiting scrap or conversion in 1892, were standing on The Dump sidings whereas those were actually on specially laid sidings immediately west of Rodbourne Road, the then boundary of the works westwards – in fact these sidings were on the site of the later A Shop, the first part of which was opened in 1902.

After running alongside the West End Rec. the Wootton Basset Road passed under the main line bridge, then the end of The Dump sidings which were almost at right angles to the road, and on built-up ground some fifteen feet higher, and then passed under the even higher red brick arch which carried the Midland & South Western Railway Section. The M.S.W.J. line was, at that point, still gaining height to pass over the G.W. main line by a further bridge. From the roadway between the two bridges it was possible to see any engines that were standing against the stop blocks on The Dump sidings and, by standing on a gate that led into some allotments in the triangle between the two sets of running lines, it was sometimes possible to see the number of the second engines in the lines.

When I first visited here regularly in 1926 I recall one diminutive engine resting against a stop block for several months. This was an 0–4–0 saddle tank, formerly Taff Vale Railway, that carried the G.W. number 1342. It had a long narrow stovepipe chimney, and saddle tanks so small that there was barely room for the G.W.R. number plate to be bolted to them, whilst the cab sheeting looked distinctly home-made. I discovered later that this had been the pilot at the Taff Vale's West Yard loco works in Cardiff for a number of years but was sent to Swindon late in 1925 and put in the 'Factory Pool', as The Dump was officially called. It was examined and condemned in August 1926, and cut up the following month; I saw it standing against the stop block, on countless occasions between Easter and September 1926.

Immediately on the north side of The Dump lay a couple of sidings used solely for the scrapping of engines out in the open, also for stabling wagons to take away the scrap. For some reason there was no direct connection between The Dump sidings and the scrap road, the connecting points being almost half a mile distant, almost directly opposite where the brick wall joined the wooden fence at The Boards. About five engines were selected from The Dump each fortnight for breaking up, and this meant a considerable amount of shunting work. This was undertaken every second Wednesday afternoon by the East End pilot, whose work seemed to cover all engine shunting at the works except in the A Shop yard.

I would go to The Boards before afternoon school to see the pilot go down to The Dump sidings at about a quarter to two. From the

classroom at Westcott School I could hear the herculean efforts of the
ancient saddle or pannier tank as it struggled with the rows of
locomotives on The Dump. It seemed as if someone in the office
always listed engines from different rows, and generally near to the
stop blocks at the end of lines, which meant moving almost a whole
line of engines each time. The exhaust from the pilot was deafening
all over the west of the town, and many times the driver obviously
had to give up, and halve the load, before it could get moving. That
not only prolonged the job, but a temporary home had to be found
for half of a line of locos, before it could go back and collect the
others. The heaving, tugging and bellowing went on throughout the
afternoon, whilst I had to sit quietly at my desk supposedly absorb-
ing events some several centuries old, while history I was interested
in was being enacted only a few hundred yards from my
classroom. . . .

It was rare that the sorting-out was completed by the time school
finished about 4.15 p.m., hence I was usually perched on top of The
Boards in ample time to see the pilot emerge from behind the trees at
the west end of the Timber Yard, towing its string of victims towards the points for crossing over to the scrap road. After pushing
the engines the half mile to their final resting place, the pilot would
quietly amble back to its stabling point at the main reception sidings,
in front of the C.M. & E.E.'s offices. By that time it was nearly five
o'clock and the day's work was over.

On the scrap road, the engines were cut up bit by bit as they
stood, a burner's torch being the principal item of equipment, whilst
large iron castings such as cylinders were smashed into pieces by a
large steel ball which was dropped on to the casting from a magnetic
crane. This was another noise that could be heard all over the west
end of Swindon for long periods. The crane driver would cut off the
power and release the ball to drop on to the casting, after which you
could hear a large magnet and its chains being lowered to pick up the
ball, which was raised to the required height again. That went on
over and over again, and could be heard for a radius of at least three
quarters of a mile.

The Dump sidings and the scrap road were barely visible from any
public place. The three sidings nearest to the main line, which we
will call Nos. 1 to 3, were at this time reserved for condemned carriages, and that effectively obliterated a view of the engines, which
were on any of the other fifteen roads. The east end of The Dump
could not be seen at all except from the end of the A Shop, whilst all
that could be seen of the west end was the view from Wootton Bas-

sett Road already described. On the far north side of The Dump was the Saw Mill area, with the M.S.W.J. line skirting the boundary. This almost complete isolation was probably the reason for some of the fascination of The Dump, coupled with the fact that most of the engines there had to be seen as quickly as possible, as when their turn came on the Wednesday afternoon, they would never be visible again.

There was, however, one place where a reasonable panoramic view over the engine side of The Dump and the scrap siding could be obtained and that was from the top of the embankment of the M.S.W.J. line adjacent to the red brick arch. From there the rows of engines could be seen, although apart from those on No. 18 siding, only the chimneys, domes and cabs were visible. The scrap siding could be seen quite clearly, but only at a distance of some 300 yards; even so the types of engines on that road were clearly identifiable, although not the actual numbers of course. In those days, name and number plates were normally left on to the last, until the splasher or cab side was being burnt off. When taken off, the plates were neatly stacked nearby, Nos. 0 to 99 in one pile, 100 to 199 in another and so on. When I first saw the piles of number plates, there were several hundred there, probably dating back to 1920 or even before, and these certainly went back a few years as there were one or two Dean 'single' plates included.

The Dump has generally been thought of solely as a scrapyard by most enthusiasts, but in the early years following Grouping it was used more for storing engines than as a temporary location for withdrawn engines till they were cut up. Immediately the smaller companies came under G.W.R. control, Swindon sent out inspectors, particularly boiler inspectors, to examine those companies' engines. Acting upon their reports, quite a large number were immediately taken out of traffic and sent to Swindon for more detailed examination. At the same time Swindon Drawing Office staff studied each class on the constituent lines to ascertain which would be suitable to be fitted with G.W. standard boilers, and whether further types of standard boilers were necessary for that purpose. This resulted in a further number of such engines, those due for heavy repair, also being sent to Swindon for experiment in this field. On top of that, some older constituent engines, which normally would have been repaired or cut up at the former company's own workshops were also sent to Swindon for scrap. All these extra engines arriving in Swindon in 1922 and 1923 put a strain on both the works and its siding capacity, resulting in a large number of them being sent to

The Dump sidings until the Works could attend to them.

By 1925 the position had eased somewhat, although there were still quite a few that had been around the works and yards in pieces for two years or more. Generally speaking, these consisted of 'one-offs' from the very small companies, where small G.W. standard engines could be sent in replacement. Three of the engines from the Llanelly & Mynydd Mawr Railway were at Swindon for a very long time, No. 339 for three years and ten months, No. 803 for just over four years, whilst No. 312, which came to Swindon on 19 February 1923, did not return to service until 29 July 1927. Whilst that was exceptional, there were twenty-three cases where engines from the Welsh lines were at Swindon for over three years before returning to traffic.

As The Dump thinned out early in 1925, so it quickly filled up again later that year when many of the eighty R.O.D.s, purchased from the War Disposals Board, were stored there whilst the sorting-out was in progress. Also in 1925, but more particularly in 1926, a number of old Rhymney Railway outside-framed 0–6–0 and 0–6–2 saddle tanks arrived on The Dump. These were sent to Swindon from the old Cardiff Docks shed, where they had been assembled from other sheds, in groups of about four at a time, being routed via Gloucester. Because of this I never saw any actually arriving at Swindon, but they went straight to the main reception sidings from where, the following morning, the pilot pushed them down to The Dump. What was particularly fascinating about these engines was their heavy slotted outside frames and, with the side rods taken off for the long journey to Swindon, the cranks were flailing about at all angles as they slowly moved towards The Dump. Four or more of these engines coupled together, giving twelve or fifteen cranks rotating aimlessly, was a sight never to be forgotten, and one which started my interest in South Wales railways in general. Most of the Rhymney engines mentioned carried very low G.W.R. numbers, between 84 and 148, and this added to their fascination as they were in the same number series as *Viscount Churchill* (No. 111) and the three French compounds (Nos. 102–104).

Although it was assumed that these engines had been called in for scrapping, I learned afterwards that they had been sent for possible repair or rebuilding, although in the event all were later condemned following examination. A few of the other 0–6–2 saddle tanks were converted to pannier tanks at Caerphilly later, but none were dealt with similarly at Swindon. There were also a few standard G.W. engines stored on The Dump late in 1925 and for part of 1926, the two I remember best being Aberdare class 2–6–0 2677, which was there for nearly a year, and Saint class 2912 *Saint Ambrose*, which was there for a few weeks in the summer of 1926. I know I was particularly surprised to see a Saint there.

Towards the end of 1926 The Dump sidings were also used for yet another purpose – the storing of engines after withdrawal for possible sale to collieries and industrial concerns. The depression which followed the General Strike of May 1926, and the accompanying lengthy miners' strike, caused the G.W.R. to take 46 engines out of traffic as from 30 October 1926. These were practically all constituent engines from South Wales, and no less than 37 were placed on a newly-created Sales List, and these were stored on The Dump. The total included thirteen of the old Rhymney 0–6–2 saddle tanks but at least four, possibly more, had already been in store on The Dump for over twelve months prior to this summary withdrawal. More engines were added to the Sales List later in 1926 and also during 1927, but as few were actually sold The Dump began to fill rapidly again. By early 1928, when large numbers of G.W. standard engines were being withdrawn, including larger ones such as 4–4–0s of the City and Flower classes, plus of course the rejected fifty R.O.D.s, the sidings became so full that it was necessary to reduce numbers by taking a number of engines off the Sales List, and cutting them up. This was started in February 1928 and, not surprisingly none of the Rhymney 0–6–2 saddle tanks had been sold, all being cut up later in the year.

Out of that 30 October 1926 mass withdrawal, one that did survive was ex-Taff Vale 0–6–2T G.W.R. No. 450, which went to Longmoor (then Woolmer) Military Railway in December 1927. It still survives, 54 years later, at the Caerphilly Railway Society's yard a mile or so from where these notes are being written. I certainly did not think that the engine I saw as a lad of nine, and which seemed certain to be broken up at the time, would still be around in my retirement.

Of the other engines withdrawn and placed on the Sales List in October 1926, I particularly remember an old Taff Vale 0–6–0 saddle tank which carried the G.W.R. number 798. Like some of the Rhymney ones it had already been in store on the Dump for several months prior to that date, having gradually worked its way to the far end of one of the sidings against the stop blocks. There it stayed, gradually deteriorating externally, through sunshine, showers, fog and snow until the end of October 1928. It seemed a permanent feature of the Dump scene, and something seemed to be missing when it was finally cut up. Other engines visible from the Wootton Bassett Road for lengthy spells during the same period were two former Taff Vale 0–6–0s (Nos. 912 and 915), and one of the Rhymney 0–6–2 saddle tanks. (No. 137).

My first and somewhat disappointing visit to The Dump was made in the early evening of Bonfire Night, 5 November 1927. Hadyn Robinson and I decided on that evening to explore the sidings, although we were not sure whether the place was patrolled by a watchman. However, we thought there would be sufficient distraction for us to look around without getting caught. Unfortunately, we had not taken the weather into account, for it rained extremely hard, but about 6.30 p.m. we climbed over the railings and made our way up the slope to the sidings. We only managed to walk between two rows of engines as it was too wet to stay longer – in fact, most of the time we were on The Dump was spent sheltering in the cabs of ex-Barry Railway 0–4–4T G.W.R. No. 4, and Taff Vale 4–4–2T G.W.R. 1303. The first attracted us as it was the lowest G.W.R. number we had seen up to that time, and the second because the engine had a mass of rods and wires between the chimney, dome and cab. This was a Taff Vale auto engine used on push-and-pull trains. The system was by overhead wires, which ran from the front of the driving trailer car, where the driver had control, over pulleys fixed on top of the cars which were attached to similar wires on the locomotive. The latter passed through tubes which were fastened on both sides of the chimney and dome and thence into a box on the cab roof. In this box the two wires passed around further pulleys and down through holes into the cab itself, each wire being fitted to an end of a double regulator handle. In the driver's compartment of the car was a large wheel, grooved at the rim to take the wire. Thus by working the wheel, the driver could open or shut the regulator on the engine. This ingenious but rather Heath Robinson affair was, surprisingly, quite successful, having been in use for about twenty years before the G.W.R. introduced their own below-frame auto gear on the former Taff Vale section.

However, to a youngster brought up on G.W.R. practice, the Taff Vale 4–4–2T looked rather weird and wonderful with the fixed pipes along each side of the chimney and dome, plus loose wires hanging down the front of the smokebox and down into the bunker at the rear end. The wires were at both ends as the system worked equally well with the cars at the front or at the rear of the engine – or, if necessary, at both ends. At the time I saw this engine, wireless sets had grown out of the crystal stage into big, heavy, valve and battery sets. To get a clear sound it was necessary to have a high aerial outdoors; this consisted of a tall post at each end of the garden, the posts both having crossbars near the top. The aerial wires were fixed on each side from crossbar to crossbar. Wherever you looked around the backs of the houses there were forests of aerials, on a much larger scale than when the initial television aerials appeared.

In my youthful innocence I could not dissociate the similarity between the wireless aerials and the wires fitted each side of the Taff Vale 4–4–2T, in fact one might say it looked like a travelling wireless machine. Fortunately a few photographs of those odd-looking engines survived, which I managed to acquire many years afterwards, otherwise I would have doubted my memory of them.

For several years I kept two small souvenirs of that visit to The Dump on 5 November 1927; a small piece of broken glass from one of the cab windows of No. 4, and a steel nut which was lying on the floor of 1303.

Before leaving The Dump for a while, mention must be made of the carriages on sidings Nos. 1 to 3, as this must have comprised the greatest museum of pregroup passenger vehicles ever assembled in one collection. There were four-wheel, six-wheel and bogie vehicles, with carriages from the Taff Vale that had previously seen service on the Metropolitan and London, Tilbury & Southend Railways. There were Barry carriages that had started life on the Lancashire & Yorkshire Railway, and an inspection car of the Burry Port & Gwendreath Valley Railway that was originally built for the Lambourne Valley. There were carriages from Brecon & Merthyr and Neath & Brecon Railways that had been acquired secondhand from the London & South Western, plus some excellent bogie coaches which the Midland & South Western Railway had purchased from the Midland. There were also carriages built for the Taff Vale, Cambrian, Rhymney and Barry Railways, mainly old four- and six- wheel stock, with quite a few still in fading pre-group livery, including the company's coat of arms and original carriage numbers.

Unfortunately we did not appreciate such an outstanding collection; as far as we were concerned they were a nuisance that hid from sight the rows of engines behind them on The Dump. It is probable that carriages were stored on those three sidings as they were the longest on The Dump, about 580 yards average length each, which all told would accommodate at least 125 of the smaller type of carriage then being sent in for scrapping. The sidings fanned out away from the main line and No. 18 siding was probably not more than 280 yards in length.

The carriages were scrapped on sidings to the west of Swindon station. The bodies, being made of wood, were burnt. However a large number of bodies were sold for further use as outbuildings, whilst a few were even converted to residences. Even more were grounded by the G.W. themselves for use as yard offices, storage sheds and the like. It was due to the sale of bodies in those days that a few have been recovered in recent years for preservation. Two former Taff Vale eight-wheel non-bogie rigids were discovered side by side with an overall roof erected above the normal carriage roofs, as a holiday home at Hayling Island. These are now being restored by the Industrial and Maritime Museum at Cardiff, which stands but a couple of hundred yards from the original Taff Vale headquarters in Cardiff's dockland. Although we youngsters took scant notice of the unique collection of old carriages on The Dump, it is fortunate that the C.M. & E.E. sent his photographer down there to record the scene, and thus leave us those delightful photographs of that never-to-be-repeated collection. By about 1930, the carriages had all gone from The Dump, and the sidings were afterwards used for wagons. I never remember an engine being stabled on any of these three.

# 3
## Barnes Yard and Rushey Platt Junction

DESPITE THE ATTRACTIONS of The Dump, there was a far better place for us to watch the trains, only a few yards away. To the west of Wootton Bassett Road, immediately before passing under the main line railway bridge, there was a large timber yard, owned by the Barnes family. That was, without any doubt, easily the most comfortable, interesting and pleasant place to watch train movements in the whole of the Swindon area. A roadway ran through the centre of the yard, being closed from the main road in the evening by swinging a long white wooden gate into position, although there was a small side-gate for pedestrians. Just inside the yard on the main line side was a pile of full length tree trunks stacked until required. As long as we did not cause a nuisance, we were allowed to sit on these trunks and watch trains to our hearts' content. Opposite, on the other side of the roadway, were two large adjoining sheds with open ends facing the railway. In these sheds were stabled three steam traction engines, two of which were usually out in the day time collecting more tree trunks. If the weather was wet we were allowed to stand in the sheds, providing we did not play about on the engines. Naturally this end of the yard had its nickname, and if anyone at school asked if you were going down to The Logs that evening, we knew what was meant.

Apart from main line train movements, the yard had other railway attractions. At the top end, reached on a gently rising gradient, was the remains of the former Rushey Platt station of the M.S.W.J. There was a reverse siding towards the timber yard, which passed a milk platform, then still in daily use, before opening to two sidings which dealt mainly with coal traffic. Originally Rushey Platt had up and down high level platforms for the M.S.W.J. main line trains, and also up and down low level platforms on the connecting loop line to the G.W.R. The Low Level station had closed early in 1885 when the G.W.R. placed such a heavy price on the M.S.W.J. for the use of its line and station that the connecting service was not economic. Even so the station house and down platform were still there in the 1920s, in fact both survived until recent times. Nothing remained of the up platform, and little of the High Level station which had closed in 1905, apart from the signal box, and a short length of platform and embankment on the down side.

The G.W.R. junction for the loop line was Rushey Platt Junction. Along with the signal box of that name, this was up on the embankment immediately in front of the tree trunks mentioned at the lower end of Barnes' yard. The loop line continued past the old Rushey Platt station, climbing to join the M.S.W.J. main line a couple of hundred yards or so further south, whilst in the reverse direction the M.S.W.J. main line climbed sharply northwards through the station to pass over the G.W. main line about eighty yards or so west of the junction signal box. Hence, seated on the logs, one had a splendid view of everything on either of the two main lines, as well as of any trains using the link line.

During school holidays it was possible to watch most train movements throughout the day, hurrying home only for brief intervals for dinner (lunch) and tea. There was always something interesting to see, including engines going on trial runs after repair at the factory. There were usually two of these, sometimes three, each working day, the engines running light to Dauntsey or Brinkworth. This only applied to the tender engines and larger tanks, the shunting ones, such as the 0–4–2, 2–4–0 and 0–6–0 tanks, normally having their trials up and down outside the works. On the main line there were certain trains we specially looked out for, including two with slip carriages, both on Bristol to Paddington expresses. The first slipped a carriage at Swindon about a quarter to nine in the morning, the other at about six in the evening. The actual point of slipping was usually under the M.S.W.J. bridge, which we always knew as 'the long black bridge', so at Barnes' yard we were able to witness the initial parting before the train sped on, the carriage trailing behind and gradually losing speed until the slip guard stopped it just west of the station. There the station bunk went out to pick it up, and take it over the points to the up platform. I was told that a few years earlier, after the express had thundered through the centre road, the points were thrown over and the guard brought the slip carriage to rest in the centre of the platform, but I certainly never saw that happen. The two slip trains were usually headed by one of the Star class, but Castles gradually took over later on. There were no slip workings in the down direction as far as I remember.

About ten o'clock in the morning a pick-up goods used to come trundling down the main line from the Transfer (the G.W. goods depot at Swindon), taking the loop line at Rushey Platt Junction. In 1926/7 this was frequently headed by one of the two rebuilt M.S.W.J. 0–6–0 tender engines, 1008 or 1013. These still each carried maker's brass plates curved around the centre splasher, which from a distance looked like non-standard nameplates. Although we soon learned that it was not so, we often ran up the roadway through Barnes' yard to watch the 0–6–0 shunting the two sidings, and stand alongside it to verify that the Beyer Peacock plate was not a nameplate. By the end of 1927 both engines had been rebuilt with G.W. Standard 10 boilers, and for a while one of these rebuilds was shedded at Swindon and would take over the duty, usually 1011 or 1013. From mid-summer 1928, however, the duty was regularly worked by Dean Goods 0–6–0 No. 2564, the only one of that class that I saw work on the M.S.W.J. section between 1925 and 1931. After shunting at Rushey Platt, the train climbed the 1 in 75 single line section to Old Town station, where it shunted for a few hours before returning at about 3.30 in the afternoon, although it did not shunt at Rushey Platt on the return trip.

The next item of interest on the main line was probably the most fascinating of the day. This was another pick-up goods which left Swindon Transfer at 10.30 a.m. for Stoke Gifford yard, (where Bristol Parkway station now stands) and regularly headed by former M.S.W.J. G.W. No. 24. This 2–6–0 had been sent into factory immediately after the take-over of the M.S.W.J. late in 1923, and few expected it to survive, being such an oddity. An outside-cylinder 2–6–0, with driving wheels only four feet in diameter, certainly was an oddity as far as Swindon Works were concerned, but they altered it until they felt it was truly Westernised. A Standard 9 boiler with Belpaire firebox was fitted, plus a huge G.W. dome cover, cast tapered chimney and, naturally, G.W. safety valve and cover. The cab sides and roof were rebuilt to Swindon pattern, and the M.S.W.J. tender was replaced by a standard G.W.R. one. Despite all the effort put in to make No. 24 look like a Swindon product, it was definitely still the odd man out. As the goods train passed Rushey Platt Junction it had picked up to about 30 to 35 miles an hour, but the tiny

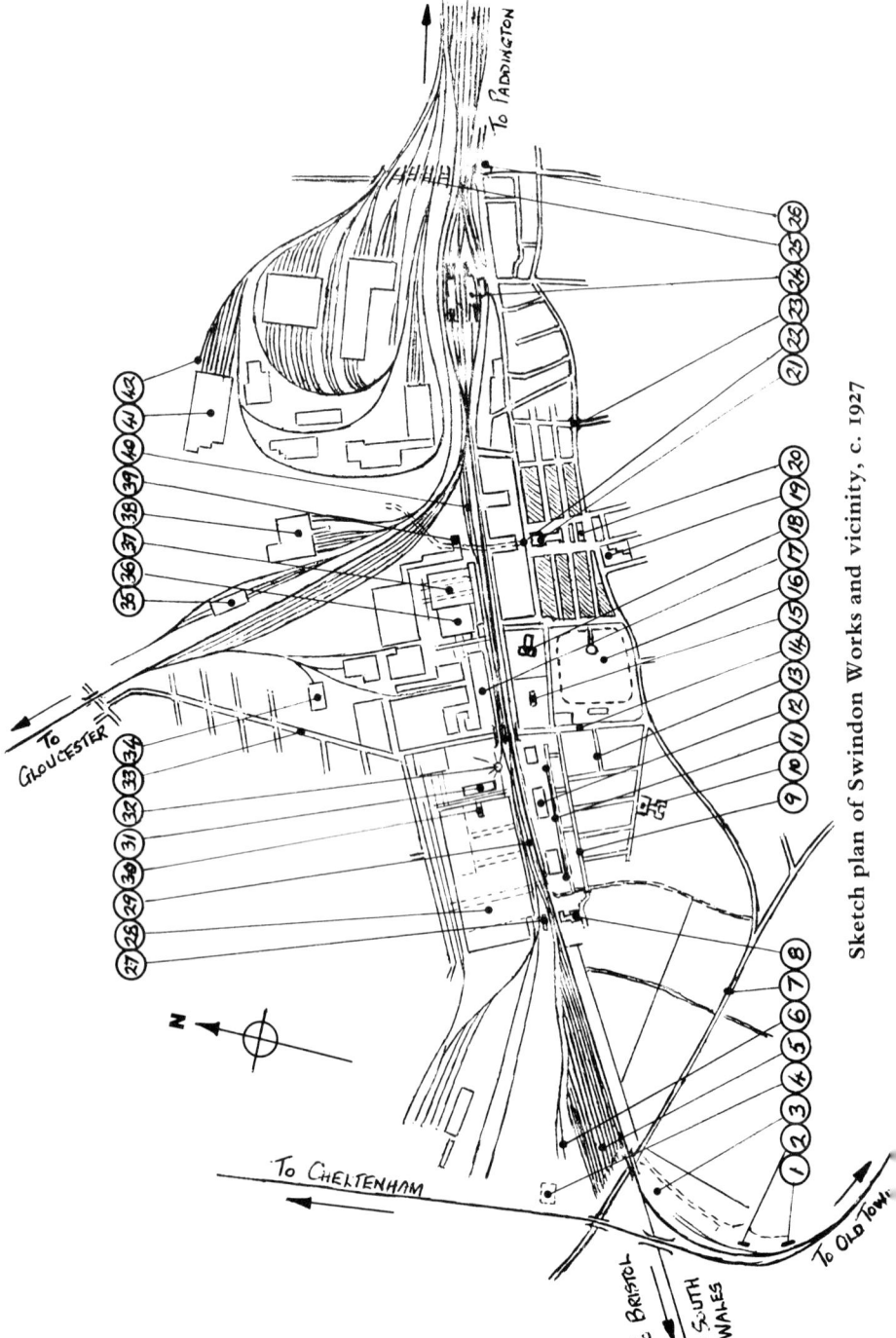

To PADDINGTON

To GLOUCESTER

To CHELTENHAM

To BRISTOL & SOUTH WALES

To OLD TOWN

N

Sketch plan of Swindon Works and vicinity, c. 1927

1 RUSHEY PLATT STATION
2 MILK PLATFORM
3 BARNES YARD (RUSHEY PLATT JCT.)
4 SITE OF NEW CUTTING UP SHOP; 1932
5 THE DUMP
6 CUTTING UP ROAD (IN THE OPEN)
7 WOOTTON BASSETT ROAD
8 NEWBURN HOUSE (G. J. CHURCH-WARD)
9 DEAN STREET
10 WESTCOTT SCHOOL
11 THE BOARDS (3 SITES)
12 TIMBER SEEDS NOS. 1 TO 3
13 JOLLIFFE STREET
14 PARK LANE
15 THE VICARAGE
16 THE PARK
17 IRON FOUNDRY
18 ST. MARKS CHURCH
19 MEDICAL FUND CENTRE
20 GWR HOSPITAL
21 MECHANICS INSTITUTE
22 THE TUNNEL ENTRANCE

23 THE CENTRE
24 SWINDON JCT. STATION
25 WHITEHOUSE ROAD BRIDGES
26 WHITEHOUSE HOTEL
27 WEIGHBRIDGE HOUSE
28 A SHOP (NEW CONSTRUCTION AREA)
29 A SHOP RECEPTION SIDINGS
30 LOCO TEST PLANT
31 THE BARN
32 TURNTABLE AREA
33 RODBOURNE ROAD
34 SPARE MACHINERY STORES
35 LOCO STOCK SHED
36 R SHOP
37 B SHED
38 LOCO SHED
39 CM & EES OFFICES
40 LOCO WORKS RECEPTION SIDINGS
41 NO. 24 CARRIAGE SHOP
42 SITE OF B & E ENGINE AS STATIONARY BOILER

[GWR HOUSES SHOWN SHADED, AROUND 21]

wheels of No. 24 were rotating at such a rate that the engine seemed to be going at least 50 or 60. We were so used to seeing the G.W. outside-cylinder 2–6–0s on goods trains which, with their 5'8" diameter wheels, seemed to be ambling along at 35 miles an hour or so.

Nevertheless we always looked forward to seeing No. 24, which was a delightful little engine and did its work well. The return from Stoke Gifford was around 5.30 p.m., and a more consistent engine on a regular main line duty I never saw. It started working the Stoke Gifford goods in February 1925 and performed the duty regularly day in and day out (weekends excepted) until withdrawal five years later. As far as I remember, the train left Swindon with about 35 wagons, and at the rear was a regular G.W. goods brake van (No. 56008) lettered 'Stoke Gifford and Swindon Local only'. No. 24 might as well have been similarly labelled during its short life on the G.W.R.

Another former M.S.W.J. engine followed just under an hour later. That was one of the two magnificent 4–4–4 tanks numbered G.W.25. It had also passed through Swindon factory in 1925, but was not extensively rebuilt and reappeared in October of that year sporting a standard G.W. parallel chimney, safety valve and – naturally – Swindon pattern cover to match. It was immediately put on the Swindon Junction to Old Town shuttle service, a service reintroduced by the G.W.R. on 22 October 1923 for the convenience of passengers changing between the G.W. and M.S.W.J. lines. The same engine, as M.S.W.J. No. 17, had worked the service until October 1924 when it was taken into factory, after which a former Port Talbot Railway 2–4–0T, G.W. 1189, often worked the duty. The train we saw regularly was the 11.23 a.m. ex-Swindon Junction station, which had hopefully waited in the Down Bay, Platform 2, for passengers changing from the 9.15 Paddington to Bristol, which called at Swindon about eleven o'clock. When I first knew the 11.23, it consisted of three G.W. clerestory bogie carriages, but this was later cut to two and, occasionally, to only one. No. 25 was allowed eight minutes for the 3½-mile journey, which headed westwards past the locomotive works until out in the countryside at Rushey Platt Junction, from where it took the loop line skirting in a semi-circle around the south western outskirts of the town before climbing the single line M.S.W.J. section to re-enter Old Town station facing, roughly, a south-east direction.

I remember No. 25 on that train so well; it always came down the main line approaching Rushey Platt Junction at a brisk rate, and took the points there whilst still running smartly. We used to desert the tree trunks when it was signalled so that we could climb the embankment to the boundary fence to watch that magical second when the front bogie would take the points – leaving, for an instant, the boiler, frame and the rest of the engine still aligned with the main line. In that split second it resembled a toy train taking the points, and the sight never ceased to fascinate me. Some 50 years or so afterwards it seems a very strange way to remember a particular locomotive and to be fair there were many other things to remember about it, particularly its rather austere outline, the massive bunker, and the sheer size of the engine in comparison to the minor duty it was performing. At Old Town the 11.23 connected with a southbound train on the M.S.W.J. and returned, bunker-first, at about noon from Old Town. Although there was a turntable at the latter it was rarely used in G.W. days, and the tank engine on the shuttle service always ran chimney-first from the Junction station and bunker-first from Old Town.

Although there was a service of about five or six trains each way daily (Sundays excepted), the early morning and tea-time services were extended to Chiseldon, three miles south of Old Town station, to pick up and return men employed at the Swindon railway works who lived in that area. Apart from those, the 1.00 p.m. train from Swindon Junction on Saturdays was extended to Marlborough – always a popular place for Swindonians to spend a few hours, the return working picking up people from Marlborough, Ogbourne, and Chiseldon who wished to spend the afternoon shopping in Swindon.

No. 25 continued regularly on that one turn until it was 'stopped' at Swindon shed on 16 April 1927. It was not condemned until October of that year and lingered on the Dump, which it had passed so many times in traffic in the previous few years, until being cut up in November 1928. Thus passed one of the engines that will always stand out in my memory. It was replaced as 'Old Town Bunk' by another former M.S.W.J. engine, the much smaller 0-4-4T G.W.R. No. 23. This had also passed through Swindon works in 1925, where it was rebuilt with a Standard No. 9 boiler with Belpaire firebox. It was an attractive-looking engine with a diminutive bunker compared with No. 25, but seemed far more suited to the light work than the larger engine had been. I do not recall seeing it working until No. 25 was 'stopped' at shed, but as the records state that it had a couple of minor repairs at Bristol (Marsh Junction) shed in 1926, it probably worked in that area for a time. However, it took over the Old Town job on a regular basis as soon as No. 25 finished, and must have gone 'Round the loop' many thousands of times before ceasing to work in December 1929; it then followed the 4–4–4T to the Dump on condemnation in February 1930.

At that time the factory was turning out a number of the small-wheeled 2–6–2Ts for suburban passenger work, and three of these engines (5558, 5559 and 5565) were shedded at Swindon direct from factory. It was one of these that took over the shuttle service from No. 23 for the next year or two. The turn was not confined to one particular engine and any of the three would work it as available. Obviously this was a minor task for a modern purpose-built sub-urban locomotive, and early in 1931 No. 5559 was transferred to the more rigorous duties of the suburban services in the Bristol area. The other two continued on the Old Town service spasmodically during 1931, but the duty was gradually left to any small engine available, usually older pannier tanks, sometimes 0–4–2Ts and occasionally 2–4–0 side tanks. In the mid-1930s I remember an old double-framed pannier tank, No. 1660, on the job for a while.

However, by that time the glamour of the M.S.W.J. workings had begun to wane, but before getting to that period I must describe the workings on the M.S.W.J. main line in the 1925 to 1930 period, before the wind of change had taken place. The first changes from the pre-group scene took place in 1924, when a few Duke class 4–4–0s were sent to the line to help work the traffic whilst a number of M.S.W.J. 0–6–0s and 4–4–0s were in factory being rebuilt or under repair. More Dukes were transferred to the line in 1925, and it was those that I remember from my first recollections of the Barnes' yard area in 1926. At that date there were about four weekday passenger workings each way over the full length of the line, Cheltenham to Andover, supplemented by one or two short distance services start-ing from Swindon Town plus, of course, the local shuttle service. There were also quite a few goods trains in both directions. Although, basically, the Dukes and the M.S.W.J. 4–4–0s worked the passenger trains, and the rebuilt M.S.W.J. 0–6–0s the goods trains, it was quite common to see the position reversed, with an 0–6–0 at the head of a passenger train passing a 4–4–0, of either class, on a goods. This often happened at Rushey Platt High Level where, with single line both north and south of the old station, it was a regular occurr-ence for both passenger and goods trains to be held up in the passing loop for a train in the opposite direction.

The Dukes on the line in 1926 were 3261 *St. Germans*, 3284 *Isle of Jersey* and 3290 *Severn*, which were at the old M.S.W.J. shed at Chel-tenham (High Street), plus 3258 *The Lizard* and 3269 *Dartmoor* which were Andover (M.S.W.J.) engines, but had spells at Swindon shed;

also 3260 *Mount Edgcumbe* which was a Swindon engine, but always worked on the M.S.W.J. section. The three shedded at Cheltenham did most of the main line passenger work originating at the northern end of the line and, despite their very Victorian appearance, carried out the duties efficiently. The Andover engines were often on goods workings, whilst 3260 seemed to be the odd-job man, on either short-distance passenger or goods work, plus the strange passenger-cum-milk local trips shortly to be described. This engine looked the most ancient of them all as it retained the original narrow cab, with the rear driving wheel springs above the curved framing outside the cab sides. This meant the number plate was bolted much higher on the cabside than the usual position. She also had a long tapered chimney which, I thought, added to the charm of the Dukes fitted in this way.

The milk train was the highlight of the day not only for the young enthusiasts who sat on the logs in Barnes' yard, but for many other local youngsters who had heard of its fame. It was also a great train for fare-paying passengers who were in no particular hurry to get anywhere. On weekdays it set off for Cirencester in the early evening and, after the strain of covering the fifteen miles (including two stops) in 29 minutes, it was allowed about an hour to recover before setting out on the return journey. For this run the allowance was 43 minutes to Old Town, which included 25 minutes for the eight and a half miles from Cricklade, and I very much doubt if it arrived on time on many sunny Summer evenings. There was a scheduled stop at Rushey Platt on that run, which the lads from the west end of town went up the timber yard to witness.

Just before eight o'clock the train ambled up the incline to pass over 'the black bridge', and saunter down the short distance to Rushey Platt. There, after passing pleasantries with the signalman, the engine was uncoupled from the train and leisurely proceeded to the points for the low level loop line. Tender-first it would slowly run back through the low level platform and on to the siding, coming to rest against the milk van which was waiting with its load of empty churns. The local lads would be assembled on the milk platform, hoping to get a ride on the engine when it performed the reverse procedure. When there were only about half a dozen or so, we were often allowed on the footplate, but one summer evening no less than twenty eight youngsters, the driver, and the fireman all rode on 3260 the half mile or so to the points and back on the high level! Where they all perched I do not know; several were on – or in – the tender, whichever way you care to look at it. I clearly remember them climbing down from the cab, one by one, and down the embankment to the low level. Whilst all this was going on the passenger coaches were, of course, stabled on the high level, the passengers themselves aimlessly looking out from the windows and doubtless thinking, 'What a way to run a railway!'

On Sundays the service was, as might be expected, not so speedy. The milk train left Old Town at 3.20 p.m. and was allowed 35 minutes to get to Cricklade, where it terminated. After chewing straws for 55 minutes at that station, it headed back for Swindon but, as it had to pick up the milk van at Rushey Platt, it was allowed 45 minutes for the eight and a half miles. The Sunday train did not attract such a large youthful audience at Rushey Platt, as it was there at tea time, and just before we had to be spruced up for the evening service. Another factor was that we were dressed in our 'Sunday best', and woe betide you if you arrived home with grime or grease on your suit. However, the few that did manage to get to Rushey Platt on a Sunday tea time were more likely to get a footplate ride than the larger number on week days.

*Mount Edgcumbe* was not the only engine involved on that job, of course, although it was a regular. Sometimes an M.S.W.J. 0–6–0 or 4–4–0 would be on the turn, and also *The Lizard* a few times. Talking of the M.S.W.J. 4–4–0s, they were a very mixed bag by the time I knew them all. There were nine, Nos. 1119 to 1126, and 1128. Of these 1121, 1124 and 1128 had been rebuilt with Swindon Standard No. 2 tapered domeless boilers, G.W. copper-capped chimneys and polished brass safety valve covers. The cab roofs had been altered with a more pronounced curve, more in line with Swindon practice, giving the engines a very distinctive appearance. When passing over 'the black bridge', with only the boilers and cab visible, they looked identical to the 34xx series of the Bulldog class, which were mostly fitted with copper-capped chimneys at the time. The Bulldogs had outside framing, hence when the rebuilt M.S.W.J. 4–4–0s could be seen complete the difference between the two classes could readily be identified. Initially Nos. 1121 and 1128 retained coal rails at the top of their M.S.W.J. tenders, but this was later filled in with plate as per standard G.W. tender practice.

These rebuilt 4–4–0s were, in my opinion, the most handsome rebuilds carried out on constituent engines at Swindon works, even more handsome that the G.W. 4–4–0s themselves, and for a few years they were kept in a very smart condition by the cleaners at Andover and Cheltenham. Nevertheless, despite my enthusiasm for these engines rebuilt, let me quickly ad that I thought the 4–4–0s

*Former Rhymney Railway 0-6-2ST G.W. No.137 standing against the buffer stops at the west end of the Dump in the summer of 1928. The M.S.W.J. embankment can be seen in the background.*
[*Author's Collection*]

*County class 4–4–0s 3801 ('County Carlow') and 3823 ('County of Carnarvon')
being cut up on the old scrap siding alongside the Dump, 17 May 1931.*

*[H.C. Casserley]*

*The frame and wheels of the last French Atlantic, No.104 'Alliance', on the old
scrap siding, September 1928. The boiler had already been removed in the AE
Shop and the cab lowered on to the front end of the frames for cutting up.*

*[M. D. England/N.R. Museum]*

in their original condition were also impressive, particularly the two 'double-domers', as we called 1119 (Andover) and 1122 (Cheltenham). These had the normal steam dome towards the front of the boiler, whilst the second dome, which housed top feed apparatus and Ross Pop safety valves, was fitted just in front of the fire-box. As built, M.S.W.J. 31 (G.W. 1128) had been fitted with a double domed boiler, but after the 1924 rebuild of that engine already mentioned, the boiler was transferred to 1119 (M.S.W.J. 1) which, in pre-group days, had the normal single dome only.

Whilst I would not suggest that the double-domers were as handsome engines as the original design 4–4–0s they were by far the most impressive, even more so than those rebuilt with G.W. boilers. I shall always remember the regular sight of 1122 at the head of the five or six bogie coaches on the down morning Cheltenham, speeding towards 'the black bridge', and directly the driver closed the regulator, to watch the Ross Pop valves spring into action and release a head of steam. It is memories like this that make me realise why diesel or electric locos could never raise my enthusiasm. . . . .

The other 4–4–0s then still in original condition were Nos. 1120 (Andover) and 1123, 1125 and 1126 at Cheltenham, but only 1125 remained with an M.S.W.J. boiler until it was withdrawn. That one and the double-domers retained left-hand drive till the end, even though the latter pair had exchanged their unusual boilers for ordinary M.S.W.J. ones by 1932. In traffic, all the 4–4–0s, rebuilt or with single or double domes, performed the same duties, and it was just as possible to see one of the rebuilt engines working a local goods 'around the loop', as it was to see one of the original ones on an M.S.W.J. main line passenger train; or vice versa.

The further 0–6–0 tender engines of the M.S.W.J. have already been mentioned in connection with the morning goods that shunted at Rushey Platt. There were ten of these, Nos. 1003 to 1011 and 1013. The two I remember in original condition had tall, spidery, cast-iron tapered chimneys which gave them a somewhat weak appearance. Such thoughts were quickly dispelled after seeing them on heavy goods trains, which they handled with ease. They had mostly been rebuilt with Standard 10 domeless boilers by early 1927, and on returning to the M.S.W.J. section they handled the traffic, passenger or freight, as easily as the 4–4–0s. Unlike the rebuilt 4–4 0s and despite their drastic Swindonisation, there was that 'something' about their appearance that instantly indicated them as non-standard. Perhaps it was because, although the G.W.R. had hundreds of 0–6–0 tender engines, all had domed boilers, and these were the first G.W.R. 0–6–0s with domeless boilers. As with the 4–4–0s, when originally rebuilt they had polished brass safety valve covers, but short tapered chimneys. Although extremely efficient, they never had the appeal of the rebuilt 4–4–0s, which seemed to be G.W.R. symmetry at its very best. The 0–6–0s, during the period I saw them regularly – say 1926 to 1932 – always worked on the M.S.W.J. section, although there is evidence that they worked on the main line to Stoke Gifford on trial runs after rebuilding, probably on the Stoke Gifford and Swindon Local goods taken over by No. 24 in 1925, and also again in the early mid-1930s after their duties on the M.S.W.J. had been taken over by larger engines, mainly 2–6–0s of the 4300 class. By 1931 the bridges on the M.S.W.J. section had been strengthened to permit the whole route, including the Swindon loop line, to be upgraded from Uncoloured to Blue classification. This permitted Bulldog 4–4–0s as well as the 4300 class to work over the line, and led to the gradual elimination of the Dukes and former M.S.W.J. engines which had made the line so interesting during the period I knew it so well. Before leaving the 0–6–0s, I would add that in 1927 six of them were shedded at Cheltenham (Nos. 1003 to 1005, 1009 and 1010) whilst the others were mainly at Swindon, with spells at Andover shed.

One annual event heightened the interest in the M.S.W.J. line before the 1931 changes. In early Autumn, excursions were run from various parts of the G.W.R. to the Military Tattoo at Tidworth. This Tattoo lasted for a week and the excursions, which consisted of normal G.W. bogie stock, were worked into Swindon Junction station in the usual way. There the train engine came off, to be replaced by a pair of Dukes, which double-headed the train around the loop, and thence to Ludgershall, where reversal was necessary for Tidworth. There were insufficient Dukes working on the M.S.W.J. section to cover the extra traffic, and each year a number of the class were sent from the Cambrian area to be temporarily shedded at Swindon for the duration of the Tattoo. This gave us the chance to see such rarities as 3256 *Guinivere*, 3259 *Merlin*, 3264 *Trevithick*, 3270 *Earl of Devon*, 3276 *St. Agnes*, 3277 *Isle of Tresco*, 3280 *Tregenna* and 3291 *Thames*-engines which normally worked from Oswestry, Machynlleth or Aberystwyth sheds at the time. About eight to ten Dukes were temporarily transferred each year for Tattoo week.

Other rarities that graced the M.S.W.J. section in those first few years after grouping was an annual appearance of a former London & South Western T9 4–4–0 on a Swindon Works Trip Week holiday special (which will be dealt with more fully later), also – but only occasionally – one of the oft-rebuilt and generally unattractive-looking 4-4-0s of the 3521 class. The two of that class that I remember best were Nos. 3557 and 3559, both then shedded at Worcester, which put in a few appearances shortly before their withdrawal.

Little has been said so far about trains on the G.W. main line in the 1926–30 period. I suppose this is because, although a life-long Great Western enthusiast, the unusual always attracts more interest than the general run-of-the-mill. As can be imagined at the home of the G.W.R. engines, most types could be seen on normal services, although 4700 class 2-8-0s, Kings and one or two tank classes were rarely seen except on running-in turns following construction or repair. It was the South Wales expresses that I remember best, particularly those that passed through Swindon non-stop on their way to Paddington; these were frequently headed by one of the two-cylinder 4-6-0s of the Saint class, surely one of the simplest first-class passenger engines ever designed. They would hurtle past Barnes' yard at full speed with the warning whistle shrieking as they sped their twelve or thirteen bogie coaches towards the works and station. I recall with affection such engines as 2910 *Lady of Shallot*, 2911 *Saint Agatha*, 2955 *Tortworth Court*, 2985 *Peveril of the Peak*, and 2998 *Ernest Cunard* on these turns. The South Wales expresses worked from the London end usually had Stars or Castles in front, and by early 1930s the latter had taken over almost completely from both ends. However, nothing could erase the memory of those 2900s, thoroughly cleaned and with all brasswork brightly polished, speeding through Swindon on the South Wales expresses. That, to me, was the Great Western at its best; magnificent engines, beautifully maintained, looking every inch Great Western thoroughbreds that were second to none.

The Paddington to Bristol and Weston-super-mare expresses were usually headed by the four-cylinder Stars or Castles, whilst local stopping trains to Bristol or Westbury, when not being used as a running-in turn for repaired engines, usually had a Bulldog or 4300 class 2-6-0 in front. Trains from Westbury usually had Bulldogs, which I always regarded as the typical G.W. engine of an earlier era. I particularly liked those with cast-iron tapered chimneys and curved footplating over the driving wheels, especially those with a combined name and number plate on the cabside (i.e. a Ringer). 3326 *Laira*, 3336 *Titan* and 3340 *Camel* were three regulars that fitted my ideal specification. In the 1920s most of the Bulldogs in the 3300 series had tapered chimneys, whilst those in the 3400 series mainly had copper-capped parallel chimneys, which made them look more modern but, to me, less attractive.

Mention of Ringers calls to mind one incident at Barnes' yard in late Autumn 1927. There was a goods train that passed down the main line about tea time. This was obviously worked by a Swindon engine, as occasionally one that had been sent in for repair was used on it for a few days before it was handed over to the works. At that time sharp inroads were being made into the Badminton class 4–4–0s and for two or three days 4136 *Terrible*, from Banbury, worked the turn prior to withdrawal. No. 4136 was a Ringer and, as the train approached the Logs, the fireman glanced out and saw the small group of juvenile enthusiasts waiting with notebooks and pencils ready. With a broad grin, he produced a large sack, which he carefully held over the combined plate with both hands as the engine slowly went by. Fortunately we had seen the same engine on the same turn the previous day, and were also just able to confirm the engine number from the front bufferbeam; hence we were able to have a chuckle back at the fireman. The following year I saw in the G.W.R. Magazine that the plate was amongst those put up for sale. Few wanted engine plates in those days, not even at £1 each, and over thirty five years later, I saw that same combined 4136 *Terrible* plate fixed on the wall at the new Swindon Railway Museum – where, I presume, it still is.

I skirted around the difficulty of reading the engine number on the front bufferbeam. When engines were ex-factory and the beam had been freshly painted red, the numbers were easy to read. However, after an engine had been out in service for two or three years, the red became almost black, or at least dark brown, and the numbers were often either not visible at all, or you would only make out one or two of them. That is one instance where I raise my hat to the old Midland Railway for providing front numberplates on the smokebox doors, although by the time G.W. engines did get the benefit of that in early Nationalisation days, it had already been nullified by fixing large reporting numberplates which obliterated the engine number there.

Returning to Barnes' yard, it was not unusual to see any of the recognised classes of goods or mineral engines working those turns. The heavy goods trains were usually headed by 2–8–0s of the 2800 class, and some by the R.O.D.s, whilst the 4300 2–6–0s were frequently a fast goods. Coal traffic from South Wales was still mainly headed by Aberdare 2–6–0s, although the 2800s also did a lot of that work. It was nothing unusual to see 4–4–0s of the Duke, Bulldog and Flower classes on goods trains – though usually fairly short distance hauls. Nos. 3267 *Cornishman*, 3272 *Fowey* and 3285 *Katerfelto* were three Dukes I remember on main line goods. The Flowers and Cities I saw on goods trains were usually working out their time prior to withdrawal. We rarely saw an engine of the City class at Swindon, except when they came in for factory attention or withdrawal.

The old outside-cylinder 4–4–0 Counties were an odd bunch, and about the only G.W.R. loco class that I remember frequently slipping when getting away from a dead stop with a load. Although I never saw one on any of the principal express trains, they would turn up on anything else, fast or slow, and occasionally even on goods work, to which they seemed entirely unsuited. There were usually at least three shedded at Swindon; in 1927 Nos. 3803 *County Cork*, 3810 *County Wicklow*, 3817 *County of Monmouth* and 3838 *County of Glamorgan* were there. They certainly took Reading trains, and I believe, some Paddington turns, whilst westwards they ran to Bristol and Weymouth. I do not remember seeing one on the Gloucester line at all. They seemed entirely out of place on goods work and I suspect they were only given that when a more suitable engine was not readily available.

The Aberdares, along with the 2–4–2 tanks of the 3600 class, which we rarely saw except en route to or from factory, were the only G.W. engines left with steam reversing gear. The lever in the cab was very small compared with the huge reversing lever fitted to many G.W. engines. As far as I remember it was normally in the mid position, and for reversing was pushed forwards and then back to the mid position, or the opposite if backward movement was required. This movement of the lever was always accompanied by the sound of a huge gush of steam, which could be heard at least 150 yards away.

Another frequent sight in those far-off days was a goods train with a small engine, out of steam, coupled behind the train engine. This was usually an 0–4–2 or 0–6–0 tank engine being sent in for factory attention, and it always carried an ordinary label tied with string to one of the upright cab handrails, stating the shed it had come from. Occasionally it might be a privately-owned engine in transit, and I recall one such 0–6–0 saddle tank, belonging to the Slough Trading Estate, heading eastwards in one train. Presumably it had received attention at either Avonside or Peckett works at Bristol. The new 0–4–0 tanks which the Avonside company built for the G.W.R. for use at Swansea Docks, were also sent from Bristol to Swindon by the same method for their G.W.R. examination and test, but it was usually just any small G.W.R. engine being sent from afar to Swindon for repair. The outside rods were removed for these journeys, and were normally stored in the bunker of the engine.

# 4

## *Swindon Works, 1927*

It was in April 1927 that I paid my first visit to the Locomotive Works. Despite my passion for steam engines I had been unable to go before this because of an official age limit, twelve I believe, imposed on visitors to the works. I had attained the ripe old age of ten that month and, being a big lad for my age, decided to try my luck. The practice in those days was that organized parties could be shown around at any normal time by prior written arrangements, whilst on Wednesday afternoons a guided tour was available to anyone who turned up at the works main entrance in London Street, always known locally as the Tunnel Entrance. I think the admission price was sixpence (2½ p) for children and one shilling for adults. I stood there with about thirty other people, both adults and children, and just before two o'clock one of the Works watchmen (who acted as guides) came outside, marshalled us into a queue, and we passed through the small side door and into the watchmen's office just inside (where it still exists exactly the same today). There the cash was collected, and anyone with a camera had it confiscated (to be returned as one left) and we set off down the long tunnel. This was, and still is, the subway below the main lines and the numerous works sidings at that point. At the end of the first tunnel, a second one followed immediately which passed below the Gloucester line and more sidings, leading to the engine shed; we turned up the slope and into the Loco Works itself. Railway enthusiasts were immediately rewarded as the first shop one went into was the B Shed, where smaller engines and tenders were repaired. Unlike other workshops in the Loco Works, B Shed was always known as 'shed' by the locals. This was because two bays adjacent to the main line, at right angles to the rest of the shop, originally comprised the broad gauge engine shed, which had become part of the factory when a new running shed was erected alongside the Gloucester line. This link with the past was also retained in my working days at Swindon, despite the two bays having been demolished late in 1929. One bay of the main shop was devoted to the repair of tenders, the other to engines, and down the centre of each bay ran a traverser table which fed the pit roads on each side; here the engines or tenders stood whilst under repair.

The pit roads were long enough to take two small tank engines, although normally only one engine or tender was allocated to each pit. The visitors were conducted down the traverser road, some youngsters usually working feverishly with pencils and note books to get down the numbers of the engines on each side. Some of these were stripped down to the bare frames, with the engine number chalked somewhere on the frame, and we youngsters would leave the main body of visitors to try to find out the number. This was frowned on by the guide, but as long as you were quick and did not hold up work or the progress of the tour, a blind eye was usually turned. In most cases the fitters working on the engine would call out the number to you to save the trouble of going between the pit roads.

After leaving the B Shed, notebooks were put away whilst the party visited the large R Machine Shop next door. Not being old enough to appreciate the skilled work carried out on the numerous lathes, planers, shapers and various other machines, I stood mesmerised looking at the hundreds of drive belts which, in whatever direction I looked, were running around the machine pulleys at the lower end, and up and around pulleys on the shafting rotating amongst the roof members. There seemed to be miles of shafting rotating up there amongst the girders. R Shop seemed one huge area of rotating pulleys and revolving belting, driving all those varied machines that were turning, shaping and boring various components.

Leaving the R Shop, on the west side one passed out into a small yard where there was a further traverser table and accompanying side roads, on which two or three small locos were assembled. Minor rectification work was carried out on those roads after an engine had been on its trial run, although in later years I saw other small engines stabled there, sometimes those on the Sales List. After crossing the traverser road and still heading westwards, the party passed into the iron foundry, known as J Shop, where the workmen were waiting to show us how white-hot molten metal was poured into sand-surrounded moulds to make the numerous iron castings required throughout railway working. At the west end of the shop we were shown the welcoming address, cast in iron, which was made in the foundry during the visit of the King and Queen in April 1924, already mentioned.

We left the foundry at the south-west corner, passed over the smaller of the two Rodbourne Road bridges and there before us was the main locomotive yard which earlier that day I had been peering at through the gaps between the timber sheds, from The Boards. However, visitors were not taken around the yard. We passed the turntable area with its radiating roads, and saw three or four engines having their post-trial rectifications. Then came a long narrow building known as The Barn. This was on the east side of yet another traverser table road, and inside were about a dozen pit roads, on which a few locos were usually stabled prior to going into the A Shop, which stood on the west side of the traverser. That traverser table, from my observations, dealt more with boilers on boiler trolleys, and wagons of components, than it did with engines. I never knew the purpose of The Barn. In those days I thought it had probably once been a Paint Shop for engines from the A Shop, but some years later I read that it was intended as a Stripping Shed for engines before entering the main shop. Whatever it may have been used for earlier, its use in the late 1920s was to carry out odd jobs on engines that did not justify occupation of valuable pit space in the A Shop.

Next we passed into the massive A Shop itself, initially through an area where there were large sections or components of locomotives, such as boilers, the front end of frames complete with buffers and buffer beams, cylinder castings and such like. These were scattered around the first of three traversing table roads within the shop. The second was more interesting, as that area covered Light and Intermediate repairs to larger engines. Boilers were not normally taken out of the frames in that section, hence the engines were more or less complete, although usually all – or some – of the wheels had been removed, and the engine often rested on large wooden blocks. From the enthusiast's point of view all number plates, and usually name plates, were still in position and, although it was not part of the visit to walk up and down that traverser road, the guide usually paused awhile while we jotted down the numbers of the thirty to forty engines in that section. They usually ranged from 4300 2–6–0s to Stars and Castles; these engines were not normally repainted after repair, just thoroughly cleaned down with paraffin-soaked rags.

After the Light Repair section we passed on to the third and largest traverser table area where all major G.W. engines received their Heavy and General repairs and where, on the pits towards the north-west corner, all new engines were constructed. Although I was un-aware of it, probably the frames of *King George V* would have been laid in the A Shop by that time, but even if they were I should not have detected anything special about a pair of frames which probably only had 'Lot 243' painted on them for identification. In other parts of the factory, components could be seen marked with Lot Nos. only, and whilst it was known this meant they were for new con-struction the Lot Nos. meant little in relation to engine classes to the young enthusiast of those days. Whilst I cannot remember any large engines under construction during that visit, I do recall seeing a new 2–6–2T carrying the number 5500, almost complete. To me that meant a new number series of which I had no previous knowledge, and it made the visit more than worthwhile. After walking around the 50 or 60 engines under repair, the half a dozen or so new ones in various stages of construction, and others, I reckoned that I had seen about one hundred engines in the A Shop that day. That total prob-ably included a few of which only the frame, without boiler or wheels, was standing on blocks over a pit road, and may have even included the odd number plate or two that could always be seen on the top of the fitters' work benches here and there, freshly painted and polished waiting to be put back.

After having our fill of the engine repair section of the A Shop, known separately as the AE Shop, we passed into the western-most end of the building where wheels were being repaired. We were shown them being re-tyred, this being achieved by heating the tyre in a circular frame of gas jets until it had expanded sufficiently to pass over the wheel skeleton, where it was allowed to cool and con-tract to form what was virtually one solid ring. Even so, the tyre was further secured by a safety ring, or key. This section of the shop was known as the AW, although there were no partitions between it and the AE section. The highlight of the AW Shop was the wheel balancing machine, where the repaired wheel and axle set was spun around at high speed, with adjustments made until the balance was perfect.

From the north end of the AW Shop, we turned eastwards on the return half of the tour. Passing along the back end of Heavy repair section, we next came to the AV Shop where boilers were repaired, and then into the AM Shop, another large machine and fitting shop. That was sited more or less at the rear of Nos. 1 and 2 traverser bays,

with the overhead AM Shop offices between. The shop was somewhat similar to the R Shop except that, whereas the latter was more
square, the AM Shop was rectangular. If my recollections are correct, some of the machines in the AM Shop had been fitted with
individual electric drives, thus to some extent cutting down the
number of belts, pulleys and overhead shafting.

Coming out the east end of the AM Shop, we next entered a boiler
yard where a number of boilers were standing. Mostly these were
awaiting entry to the boiler shop for repair or, in one or two cases,
they had been repaired, tested and were waiting to go back on an
engine. Each boiler had its number painted on the side at the front
end, and often an engine number would be painted below, i.e.
Bxxxx above and Exxxx below. Occasionally a youngster jotted
down the boiler number by mistake, causing a minor headache later
trying to find an explanation for a number which did not exist in the
loco series. As a considerable number of boilers carried numbers fairly similar to engines, I now wonder how many of my early engine
lists contained the occasional boiler number. It does not really matter, however, as all my early engine notebooks have long since gone,
and one has to rely solely on memory for those far-off, but particularly interesting, days.

At the east end of the Boiler Yard was the P1 Shop, the boiler
mounting and steaming shop. This was a large workshop where
boilers were tested under steam and hydraulic pressure, and finished
off ready to go back on the engines. From the P1 Shop we walked
down a slope and passed under Rodbourne Road, rising again to the
deafening noise of the main Boiler Shop, or V Shop. It was there
that heavier repairs to boilers were carried out, and new boilers constructed. Alongside the pedestrian route below Rodbourne Road,
there was also a novel passage for boilers being transferred from the
V to the P1 Shop. They were mounted on trolleys, taken down a lift
from which they moved over a short length of underground rail
track to another lift, and this took them up to the testing shop.

In the Boiler Shop itself the noise was shattering, just as if all hell
had been let loose. Whether this was normal, or some of it put on for
the visitors' benefit, I do not know, but the sound of dozens of rivetting hammers pounding against the hollow boiler shells was one you
never forgot. You could not hear anyone speak even if they shouted,
and everyone put their hands over their ears. It must have been a
terrible place to work in, and it was hardly surprising that all the
boilermakers from there that I knew, were either deaf or partially
deaf, despite always having cotton wool in their ears whilst working.

After these noisy few minutes watching the various processes in the repair of boilers, we passed out from the north-eastern corner of the shop into the open air, and across yet another traverser road. After a brief visit to the L2 Tank Repair Shop on the other side, we went in to see work in progress in the Points and Crossings (X Shop) and the Rolling Mills (which never carried a letter classification as did most of the other workshops).

The last call was to the Steam Hammer Shop, also not classified, where we watched the hammermen's skill in pounding huge slabs of red-hot metal into the required shapes by means of delicately balanced power hammers. After a few strokes from the hammer you saw a length of steel being formed into a locomotive connecting rod. However, the highlights of a visit to this shop was that the guide borrowed a pocket watch from one of the visitors (wrist watches being little worn in those days) and handed it to one of the hammermen who placed it, glass side up, on the huge steel block beneath a 5-ton hammer. He then brought the hammer down until it appeared to be sitting on the watch glass, with just a few thousandths of an inch between the glass and the hammer. With the visitors suitably impressed, the hammer was then raised and the watch returned to its relieved, but admiring, owner. Over the next five or six years I watched the skill of the hammerman at least three or four times every year on visits, and never once did I see a watch glass broken.

The visitors left the Steam Hammer Shop, crossed a yard to the back end of the B Shed, where occasionally an engine would be stabled on one of the traverser roads outside the shop, and returned to the Tunnel Entrance by way of the corridor between the B Shed and the C.M. & E.E.'s offices. At the watchmen's office, cameras were returned to those who had brought them, not aware of the rule, and we were once again back out in London Street. Enthusaists had had a good sixpennyworth and, with luck, would have seen up to about 150 engines, whilst the 'grown-ups' in the party had seen the men and their skills that produced the finest locomotives in Great Britain – or indeed anywhere else at that time.

It will be noted that the Carriage and Wagon workshops were not visited at all. These shops were classified by numbers, not letters as in the Loco Works. There were probably several reasons why they were not included; firstly they were mostly some distance away on the far side of the Gloucester line, whilst the Carriage Shops close to the Tunnel Entrance were on the opposite side of the main line to Bristol to the Locomotive Shops, the main line running through the

*Name and number plates from scrapped engines in the C Scrap Shop circa 1937. Discernible are combined plates 3343 'Camelot' and 3349 'Lyonesse', together with 'Sir Lancelot' (3302).*

[Author's Collection]

*Siding No.1 on the Dump in 1925, with absorbed carriage stock that had been condemned.*                                    *[British Railways]*

*Rushey Platt station looking south, September 1961. Note the Low Level down platform (closed in 1885) still in situ.*          *[Author]*

railway works at that point. As the Loco Works were self contained in the triangle between the main and Gloucester lines, it was far more convenient for the two and a half hour afternoon tour than the more scattered Carriage and Wagon shops.

Whilst that remained the general pattern of the regular Wednesday afternoon visits, the immense interest in Swindon Works created by the publicity of *King George V's* successful visit to the centenary exhibition of the Baltimore & Ohio Railroad Company in U.S.A. resulted in vastly increased visits to the works. Even prior to the return of 6000 from America, and the further publicity when it first hauled the Cornish Riviera Express, the demand for visits to Swindon necessitated regular excursions being run from Paddington, and soon afterwards from other large towns and cities on the G.W.R. The first of these were two half-day excursions from Paddington on 3 November 1927, a King being provided in each case as a bonus. The first was headed by 6001 *King Edward VII* and the second by 6003 *King George IV*. For five shillings per head the people who joined those first excursions had non-stop high-speed runs for the 77.25 miles to Swindon and back, plus a conducted tour of the Works.

Further excursions soon followed and these continued for at least another ten years, although in the 1930s these mainly consisted of organised parties of school children from different areas, rather than speculative excursions. These will be referred to later on but, returning to late 1927, the authorities decided to make it more interesting by running an engine on the Test Plant for the visitors' benefit. The Plant was only occasionally used in the mid-1920s and, as it would be pure coincidence if it was in use when the visitors passed that way, it was not included in the standard tour on my initial visit in April 1927.

The Plant was sited mid-way down the east end of A Shop, on the opposite side of the traverser road to the Barn. Instead of using any engine that happened to be available for the visitors, it was decided to take one out of traffic for the purpose, and 4-4-0 4113 *Samson* was chosen. This member of the Badminton class was shedded at Oxford and was doubtless chosen partly as it had 6'-8½" diameter driving wheels (to show off the Plant to good effect) and partly because it belonged to a class due for rapid withdrawal. *Samson* was sent to Swindon on 28 November 1927 and was stabled in the Barn after its tender had been removed. It was given a thorough cleandown, but not repainted with the safety valve cover highly polished. It had a cast iron tapered chimney and, if my memory does not fail me, flat brass beading curved around the driving wheel splashers, a custom of an earlier era that had almost died out by that time.

Afterwards, whenever visitors were coming, either by excursion or on the Wednesday afternoon parties, *Samson* was lit up, and moved across the traverser table to the Test Plant. After being secured in position, and steam pressure suitably raised, she was run at high speed for their benefit, although the engine was not, of course, moving at all. The large diameter driving wheels, with their outside cranks, were an impressive sight as they turned at speed on the wheels of the Plant beneath them. This routine continued for the next couple of years or so, a period during which most other engines of the class had found their way to the scrap yard. At some stage, probably during 1929, *Samson* was repainted green including the brass safety valve cover; the brass splasher beading was removed or also painted over. Its duties on the Test Plant ceased in the early Summer of 1930 and, most surprisingly, 4113 then had a light repair at the works and was put back into traffic at Didcot shed in August. Condemned, it was back in Swindon before the end of May the next year and was sent down to The Dump sidings. For some unaccountable reason it was put on the Sales List, although it is far from clear who would be likely to come forward as a buyer of 4–4–0 passenger tender engine. Not until 1934 was it taken off this List, being finally broken up in September of that year. In the meantime the external condition of *Samson* had sadly deteriorated, but the name and number plates were retained to the last.

For a few weeks after *Samson* had been taken off Test Plant duty, it was replaced by one of the Saints, 2931 *Arlington Court*. The main thing I remember about this 4–6–0 was that the right-hand name plate looked odd. Although mounted in the usual position above the centre driving wheel splasher, the plate had no lower spacing section below the beading, thus making visible the three fixing brackets, which could not be seen on other engines. The reason for this oddity seemed to be that, for some unknown reason, the reversing rod passed between two of the brackets, whereas it passed behind on other Saints. To one brought up on G.W. standard practice, this spoiled the engine's appearance that side; fortunately when on Test Plant work, visitors always saw the left side of the engine. Although the plate that side was similar, the absence of the reversing rod made it seem more presentable. *Arlington Court* did not stay long on the job, perhaps because the Running Dept. could ill-afford to spare a first class passenger engine mainly to amuse works visitors, and it returned to traffic in the late Summer of 1930, to last another twenty years in service. After that, no further engines were kept at the works merely for Test Plant demonstration use, but when large parties of visitors were expected, any available large engine at the works would provide the show if at all possible. Even so, in 1935 *Arlington Court* was again on the Test Plant for most of the year, but on that occasion it was for a series of controlled testing, although sometimes it was made available for the larger parties of visitors who were taken round the works in that G.W.R. Centenary Year.

It should be mentioned that Swindon was so famous at this period that quite a few important people went there to see for themselves what was widely regarded as the showpiece of British railway engineering. For example, a further Royal visit was made on 21 March 1928 when King Amanullah of Afghanistan and his Queen toured the factory. However, the most spectacular visit I remember (but of which, unfortunately, I now have no details) was paid by another exalted personage from the Eastern world. He and his colourful party were dressed in long flowing robes and, apparently, it was the custom that a large, equally colourful, umbrella or sunshade should be held over him at all times when in public. This must have proved awkward at times during the visit, particularly when he climbed on to the footplate of one of the engines that had been prepared for his inspection just outside the A Shop. . . .

Another regular visitor was that most famous of all G.W.R. locomotive chiefs, G. J. Churchward, although his visits were on an entirely different basis of course to those paid by other important personalities. Churchward had retired at the end of 1921 to his home, 'Newburn', which stood in its own grounds entered from the west end of Dean Street, (named after his predecessor). From Newburn there was a private foot-crossing over the main lines and sidings to the Weighbridge House, which stood near the south-west corner of the A Shop. The word retirement hardly applied in Churchward's case – or fell on deaf ears – as, in order to keep fully abreast with locomotive development, what was going on at the works and, doubtless, to keep in touch with his former friends and colleagues, he paid frequent visits across the line to the workshops, usually at least a couple of times a week. There was an alternative works subway from the end of Dean Street to the Weighbridge House, but G.J. preferred to use his private crossing.

As a youngster I saw him on countless occasions, as in the afternoon it was his custom to go for a ride in his motor-car. I used to watch the car glide along Dean Street, with his chauffeur at the wheel, G.J. always sitting bolt upright in the back seat, taking a keen interest in all that was going on, and to my mind looking every inch an elegant Victorian gentleman. He seemed to be a lonely man; he had never married and lived in a large rambling house, set amidst trees, with four servants, the chaffeur, a housekeeper and two maids for company. It seemed little wonder that, in view of his love for steam locomotives and the factory that built them, that he paid regular visits across the line to the A Shop.

The daughter of the elderly couple who lived next door in Joliffe Street, a Miss Mabel Scrivens, was one of the two maids at Newburn. As I frequently had to run messages back and forth between Miss Scrivens and her parents, I was a regular – unannounced – visitor to Churchward's home, even if normally only to the servants' kitchen. Even so, I saw the great man many times when I was hurrying along his drive towards the house. He was well known and loved throughout the town, having been the first Mayor of the combined New and Old Towns in 1900, hence his tragic death on that wet and miserable morning of 19 December 1933 cast a gloom over the whole area.

Despite the low misty drizzle that hung over the lines and sidings, G. J. decided to go over to the A Shop. What actually happened after that no-one will ever know, but as he walked over the crossing in the depressing gloom, he was knocked over and killed instantly by the 8.55 a.m. express ex-Paddington, headed by 4085 *Berkeley Castle*. It is possible that he was engrossed in thought and his concentration left him momentarily or perhaps he simply did not see the approaching train. In any case, an open verdict was recorded at the inquest but, despite a few mutterings, no-one in Swindon really contemplated the possibility of suicide by the genius who loved and lived for steam engines. His will favoured many charities with which he had been associated, and also revealed his thanks and generosity to his servants, who had been with him for a long time. Although I knew, when watching his funeral procession, that this was the passing of a great man, it was many years afterwards before I realised that we were actually saying farewell to the greatest British locomotive engineer of his day, one whose name will always be remembered whenever, and wherever, steam locomotives are discussed.

# 5

## *Schooldays, 1928–30*

RETURNING TO EARLIER boyhood days, I was accepted as a choirboy at St Marks Church in 1927. In those days the churches were always well filled, and there was keen competition for a place in the choir. The church is well known to rail travellers and enthusiasts as it stands alongside the main line, opposite the (then) east end of the iron foundry, having been built there in 1845, on land provided by the G.W.R. It was still considered the 'railway' church in my young days, although that was not strictly true of course, despite its long railway tradition and associations. In fact the last C.M. & E.E. of the G.W.R., F. W. Hawksworth, was a regular member of the choir until his death a few years ago.

Swindon people were divided whether they liked, or disliked, the form of service then in use. St Marks was a high Church, with much of the trimmings of the Catholic faith, such as confessions and the burning of incense. The other principal church in the town was the Parish Church, or Christ Church, on the hill up towards Old Town. That was a Low Church, with the more simple services that many people preferred. Hence the faithful in Swindon were, in a friendly way, split between the High and Low Church.

As I was brought up from infancy by the teachings of St. Marks, it was natural that when the time came I should endeavour to join the choir there. As a bonus this gave me access to a couple of excellent places to pursue my railway hobby. At the back of the churchyard was another tall timber boundary fence where, at the east end, stood the works' fire station. This had a low, sloping roof on which, by climbing up the last support post, you could half-sit, half-lie and watch the trains at close range. Its advantage over The Boards was the uninterrupted view of the railway scene – anything passing on the main line, engine movements in the vicinity of the B Shed although only a long-distance view of the A Shop yard.

One of my first recollections from the Churchyard, as we naturally nicknamed the spot, was of the East End pilot pushing No. 2177 down to the Dump. It was an outside-framed 0–6–0 saddle tank, formerly Brecon & Merthyr No. 1 which had arrived at the main reception sidings the previous day. By that date, January 1928, the days had already gone when four or five old Welsh engines would be pushed to The Dump coupled together, although it was a regular daily occurrence for at least five engines which had arrived for repair to be towed by the pilot from the works reception sidings to the A Shop area. There they were left on a siding near the running lines, but were quickly moved by the A Shop pilot, and shunted in position on the two adjacent reception sidings. Another set of engines which arrived in batches of five during the Summer of 1928 were new 0–6–2Ts, 6650 to 6699. These were built by Armstrong, Whitworth & Co. at Newcastle, part of a plan to relieve the shortage of work at various private firms due to the amalgamations of 1922–24. Previously many of the smaller railway companies had relied on these firms for the construction, and much of the repair, of their locomotive stock. This work disappeared when it was taken over by Swindon and other similar large railway workshops. Nos. 6650 to 6654 arrived at Swindon on 18 August and all ten groups of five had been received two months later. They were taken down to the A Shop yard, where they were separated and individually taken into the workshop for examination and test.

Apart from works shunters' movements, I also used to watch the non-stop expresses hurtling past the Churchyard, particularly the Slip train about six o'clock in the evening. By the time it passed the Church, the slip carriage was well behind the express, which was being slowed down for the stop at the signals approaching the station, which were sited a short distance eastward from the works' main reception sidings.

Another train that particularly interested me was a down empty milk train that went by about half an hour or so before the Slip train. A Bulldog, County or 4300 class would usually work this train, which comprised about 25 or 30 of the old wooden slatted-side milk vans. They seemed to be of all shapes and sizes, and so intrigued me that I started jotting down the van numbers as they passed. The numbers were painted on one of the wooden slats, and it was only at the Churchyard you were close enough to ascertain the numbers as they were not very large figures.

On the west side stood the Vicarage in its own grounds. Unlike the tall wooden fence at the churchyard, the railway obviously considered the same unnecessary for the protection of the vicar, and the boundary there was a much lower timber fence with a low stone wall on the vicarage side. Someone must have designed that boundary with a railway enthusiast vicar in mind, as the wall was just the right height to step up on, and the fence exactly the right height to hold on to comfortably whilst watching train and shunting movements. For convenience it was a close second only to Barnes' yard. However, as a junior choirboy I could not venture across the vicarage gardens at will to watch trains and it was usually only at the invitation of one of the young curates who was also a keen railway enthusiast. Despite his long black cassock, he frequently accompanied me to the top of the tall fence at the back of the churchyard, and no doubt some passing train travellers must have looked askance at the sight of a parson sitting on the Fire Station roof scribbling down engine numbers.

There has always seemed a close affinity between the clergy and railway engines – something that I have come across on many occasions, in vastly differing locations, over the years. Perhaps it is much the same with any other occupation or profession, and it is just that the attire makes it more prominent with the clergy. This brings to mind an incident at St. Marks a few months after I had joined the choir. Like most youngsters, I enjoyed the singing and the livelier parts of the service, but often found the sermons dry and tedious. One Sunday morning in 1928 the young curate walked up the steps of the pulpit and commenced his sermon. As usual the choirboys, after showing initial interest, either started fidgetting about or nodding off – being reasonably safe as the curate had his back to the choir. After a few minutes an approaching express could be heard belting past on the Up main with, as usual, its whistles blasting at full pitch. The curate paused in this sermon for a moment and then, in a faraway voice as if he was seeking Heaven's guidance, said, 'I wonder if that was a Castle or a King?' Naturally my ears pricked up instantly and the rest of the choir arose from the slumbers, whilst the congregation showed renewed interest, wondering what would follow. However, after another very brief pause, he carried on with his sermon without reference to that magic moment that had made my day. I never knew if he realised he had spoken loud enough for the whole congregation to hear. . . . Whatever the answer I did find out that day, that the clergy beneath those long black cassocks are as human as the rest of us.

In 1928, despite spending so much of my out of school hours watching trains, I passed the examination to go to the Swindon and North Wilts Secondary School (later called The College), which is the equivalent of a grammar school of today. This had an immediate effect on my hobby. Firstly the school was about twenty minutes walk from home, with no school buses in those days, and that meant no time to spend at mid-day looking at engines from The Boards. Secondly we were given an amount of homework which left little time to visit Barnes' yard, or other places of railway interest. On the credit side I was given my first bicycle for passing the exams, and was thus able to get to the yard or the station much more quickly.

Digressing for a moment, mention must be made of the Swindon trams, thirteen of them. They were much the same as other open-top trams of the period, that used to rattle and grind along the centre of the road with the motorman clanging his gong, or bell, at frequent intervals. There were only two tram routes through the town, one from Rodbourne to Gorse Hill which both started and terminated on the north side of the main line, but passed under railway bridges towards each terminus and for the bulk of the journey ran parallel to the railway on the south, or town, side. This went past the principal places connected with the railway, the works entrances in Rodbourne Road, the Park, then the Tunnel Entrance, G.W.R. Hospital and Medical Fund centre which were all in close proximity, followed by the Town Centre (normally just called the Centre), the station, and finally close to the football ground.

The other route started from a right-angle junction with the first route at the Centre, passed through the main shopping area to the Town Hall, thence up the steep Victoria Road to Old Town, turning from Wood Street to terminate at the Corn Exchange. There was a good service on both routes despite the few cars, but these came to a more or less abrupt stop when the time was approaching for the railway factory to cease work for the mid-day break or at tea time. At least four cars would be sent to the works' entrances in Rodbourne Road, whilst another five or so would wait in Faringdon Road, by the Medical Fund Centre, for the mass exodus of workers from the Tunnel Entrance. Allowing for the two or three cars under repair or servicing at the sheds, that accounted for the Swindon fleet.

In those days youngsters were brought up to stand in the trams if *any* adult did not have a seat, hence we normally made for the top deck – from which you had a far better view anyway. Here there were slatted wooden seats with reversible backs which you could alter to suit the direction of travel. Of course it was not much fun on the upper deck when it was raining. but it certainly ensured you a seat, and we used to enjoy watching sparks fly from the pulley connection with the overhead wires as the tram lurched and bumped along. The pulley was at the end of the long steel conductor mast; and at the terminus we would watch the tram conductor use his long wooden pole with its hook to pull the mast and the contact pulley down from the wire, and turn the lot half circle until it was at the back end of the tram for the return journey. We loved to see if he would miss when he raised the mast to again match the pulley to the wire, which he often did, and we would scatter before he howled his wrath at our chuckles. I mainly used the trams on Saturday afternoons to go to the Country Ground to watch Swindon Town F.C. play, – although generally it was the opposition that did the playing in those days – and at the end of the match there would again be four or five trams lined up to take part of the crowd away, those that could walk, or run, to the trams the quickest.

I was only twelve when the trams were abandoned on 11 July 1929. I remember watching the last one, decorated for the occasion, as it was driven around on that last day. They were noisy, cumbersome machines as they elbowed their way through the narrow streets, but were part of the Swindon scene with which I was familiar, and I knew I should miss them. A few months before the trams had gone, a few buses appeared in the town, long low single-deckers they were, to open up new routes starting from the Town Hall. They used to stand alongside the east wall of that building, and evoked much curiosity when they first came into service.

During 1928 I saw two named small tank engines that I had not seen before. We had seen 0–4–2T 1473 *Fair Rosamund* occasionally when it was sent in from Oxford for works attention. It had polished wooden nameplates on the tank sides with brass letters screwed on. However on 29 June 1928 from a works' Trip Week on holiday special, I saw 1813 *Holmwood* standing on one of the reception sidings in the A Shop yard. It was one of the large 0–6–0 pannier tanks which had spent the previous few years at Bassaleg, a former Brecon & Merthyr shed. Much later that year I was at The Boards when the pilot pushed a small 0–6–0 side tank down to The Dump. In the few seconds I saw the engine I could clearly make out the painted name on the tank side *Great Mountain* and its number 944. I had not heard of the engine before, and was surprised it was still painted a reddish-brown colour. Later I found out that it had originated on the tiny

One of the former M.S.W.J. 4–4–4Ts (G.W. No.25) in Swindon shed yard, 11 September 1927, three weeks prior to withdrawal. [H.C. Casserley]

0–6–0ST No.1397, one of the diminutive Carriage and Wagon Yard shunters, seen circa 1929. [Author's Collection]

4-4-0 No.4113 'Samson' on the test plant, circa 1920.

[British Railways]

Llanelly & Mynydd Mawr Railway and it had not been to Swindon previously. Years later I acquired a photograph of the engine, taken in 1926, and the name was not readily visible, but the word *Great* could be made out. Had I not seen the engine that October 1928 I would have thought that the words visible on the 1926 photo were *Great Western*. The shed cleaners at Llanelly must have worked hard on the engine during the two year interval, as the name was pretty clear when I saw it. For the record, *Great Mountain* was not cut up, but sold about four months later.

Soon after I had found my way around my new school, I discovered one of the greatest items of locomotive history that I had then come across. In an upstairs drawing classroom (No. A8) was assembled the complete reversing gear, valve gear and motion of that most famous of all broad gauge singles, the *Lord of the Isles*. This was not replica, but the actual gear as removed from the engine when it was broken up in 1906 after having been stored at the works since withdrawal in 1884. Although Churchward has often been criticised for scrapping both the *North Star* and the *Lord of the Isles*, in fairness it should be stated that he offered the latter to three places before it was broken up. The first two were museums, one of which was the Science Museum in South Kensington. As neither could find a home for it, he finally offered it, complete, to my old school. There was a proposal to set it up on a plinth in front of the main entrance, thus facing Victoria Road. This also fell through, although the local Education Authority, which was very railway-minded in those days, accepted the motion and gear as a working exhibit for technical training, not as a museum piece. Training a youth in the workings of a steam engine was, of course, as important in Swindon as teaching him maths or other subjects, for the vast majority of students would be connected with the railway works, in one sphere or another, in due course.

Few rooms at the schools could have accommodated the large assembly, which was set up at the rear of the classroom complete from the huge reversing lever at the back to the motion blocks at the front end. The gear was neatly assembled upon wooden stands, and at one end was a platform resembling the floor on the driver's side of the cab. Over the next few years I often mounted the platform and 'reversed' the *Lord of the Isles*. The name was stamped in full on various levers and items of motion, in the same way that engine numbers were stamped on the same parts of standard gauge locos later. At the top of the reversing lever was a short inwards side handle, for easier grip when operating the main lever and pawl. Whether that was original or not I do not know as I have never seen this on cab photographs of these old broad gauge singles.

Early in 1957 I related the story to an old friend, the late Phil Reed, who was probably the greatest expert on broad gauge locomotive history, and he was very interested to find out whether the gear was still in position. On my next visit to Swindon I paid a visit to the school and made enquiries but the staff at that time, although helpful, had no knowledge of the gear at all – indeed none could even remember it. I did hear later that it had been dismantled during the war, at which time of course, the town was changing from a hundred per cent railway environment, to having an appreciable interest in the aircraft industry. It was said the gear had been returned to the Loco Works, but how much of it, if any, survived the numerous scrap drives during the war years is not known. One other railway relic at the school was a vertical boiler, originally in use on one of the steam rail cars, still with its polished brass number plate. This was in use as a heating boiler in the small boiler house on the far side of the boys' quadrangle.

# 6

## *Swindon station and surrounds*

I HAD BEEN REGULARLY visiting Swindon station for some time, together with another good vantage point I had discovered nearby, on the pavement outside the Whitehouse Hotel on the east side of the station. From there, all train movements into and out of the station on the Paddington side could be seen, including light engines sent in steam for factory repair from the Paddington area or the Midlands. These, arriving on the Down Main, used to stop near the Station East signalbox, then reverse over to the up sidings, for a second reversal to the engine shed road. It was at the Whitehouse that we spent a lot of time as it cost one penny to go on the station platforms and regular pennies were not so easy to come by in those hard times. The station itself was a somewhat formidable-looking stone building, entered by a rather dirty and evil-smelling subway. Half way along were steps leading up to the down side platforms, and at the far end similar steps to the up side. At the top of each set of steps was a ticket snipper's box; once a platform ticket had admitted you to the side of your choice, you were not allowed to cross to the other side on the same ticket.

The two sides were spaced widely apart as, originally, four broad gauge tracks had passed between the main up (No. 5) and down (No. 4) platforms. Each side comprised an island platform, with two bays plus a relief platform. The down side relief (No. 1) was called the Gloucester platform, although a few other trains used it, especially those terminating at Swindon, also some parcels trains. The two partly-covered bay platforms (Nos. 2 and 3) were quite short, being used mainly for local and workmen's trains – to Old Town and

Marlborough (No. 2) and Wootton Bassett, Purton and Kemble (No. 3), although on occasions they swapped over. The up side bays were open (i.e. uncovered) and slightly longer, with a carriage stabling between them. The Highworth Bunk, as the branch train to Highworth was called, used either bay, but mostly No. 7, stabling its train between trips on the spare road. A stopping train to Didcot usually left from No. 6 bay, whilst later in the day a short train of L.N.E.R. carriages was stabled there. The up relief platform (No. 8) was known as the Up Gloucester being principally used for that purpose although, as on the down side, certain other passenger and also parcels trains used it. In the 1930s this was the most famous of the eight platforms, as the Cheltenham Flyer, then the world's fastest train, left from there. At the west end of the up side there were further partly covered bays, without platforms, where coaching stock was stabled for servicing between trains. On the down side there was also a long un-numbered platform, serving a dead-end siding that catered for milk traffic. Between the two sides, there was a long covered footbridge, although I never remember this being open to the public as it was used by railway staff, particularly the women who served in the Refreshment Rooms. Some of these 'lived in', with accommodation above the up side platforms.

This then was Swindon station in my young days, a hive of activity and available to us youngsters for one penny. Officially that only entitled you to stay on the platform for one hour only, the platform tickets listing each hour of the day so that the snipper could punch it correctly at the time you entered. Few did so, and usually you could stay for a whole morning, or afternoon, without any trouble.

On occasions I would save pennies until I could afford a ride in the Old Town bunk, or the 11.23 to Swindon Town as it was officially called. The fare was 2½d (about one new penny), but it was money well spent. I used to present myself at the booking office just after nine o'clock and ask for a child's single to Old Town. Without fail, the booking clerk would tell me there was no train until twenty past eleven, and that I could get a tram, across the road, at any time for a penny. However, after realising I was only interested in looking at engines and not getting to Old Town, he would issue the ticket. Thinking back, I realise he should have guessed anyway, as few passengers ever purchased a ticket between the two stations, the service being for the convenience of long-distance passengers making connections between the main line and M.S.W.J.

The ticket was my passport to two hours train watching on the down side, and a ride on that famous inter-town run known to enthusiasts as 'going round the loop'. Leaving the station, you could usually see one or two carriage and wagon shunters before spotting the engines at the main reception sidings, then pass the B Shed with smaller engines waiting shops or out after repair. Carrying on past the foundry, there were always a couple more engines on the two dead-end sidings alongside, and then you were in the A Shop area, where normally at least thirty engines were 'on view' outside the shop, either in the turntable area, around the Barn, or on the shop reception sidings. At the west end you could count on seeing one or two repaired engines near the Weigh House, followed by the line of condemned carriages that stretched the whole length of The Dump. If you were quick enough you would get a few further numbers from the engines at the west end of there, as you had a much better view of them than from the Wootton Bassett Road below. After passing through Rushey Platt Low Level station and joining the M.S.W.J. single line to Old Town, you could then sit down and study your notebook to see how many new numbers you had added that day. On arrival at Old Town station at half past eleven there was just time for the long downhill walk home to be in time for lunch (called dinner in those days), feeling that it had been well worth while. I did two or three trips around the loop behind No. 25 before it was withdrawn, but mostly behind No. 23 in 1928 and 1929; thereafter, I did it again on the final M.S.W.J. tour on 10 September 1961. Little did the G.W. realise that, when they restarted the loop service late in 1923, they had provided a service for railway enthusiasts for many years to come, being the ideal way to see the numerous engines lined up alongside the loco works.

Returning to the station, a platform ticket allowed you to study favourite engines at close range – perhaps *Guy Mannering*, *Blasius* or *Prince George*, and sometimes the drivers would let you up on the footplate - the holy of holies. And that eventually led to shunting spells on the station pilots. We called the up side pilot the Station Bunk and the down side pilot the Whitehouse Bunk, as much of its duties consisted of shunting the carriage sidings to the east of the hostelry. Riding these pilots, I soon learned that the best and quickest way to fry eggs and bacon was on the fireman's shovel. During quiet spells, the hot water pressure hose was sprayed over the blade, the eggs cracked over the rim and then emptied in. The bacon followed and into the firebox it went. In next to no time the job was done, and never were such tasty eggs and bacon produced in any other way.

I was no more than eleven or twelve years of age when I had my first real footplate ride. The driver of the Station Bunk asked me if I would like to ride to Highworth and back. Would I! If I had had £1,000 I would have willingly given it for such a ride. He told me to be on the platform on the Saturday morning, where I joined the Bunk as usual. It was one of the duties of that pilot to take an occasional run out to Highworth and back, and the engine on this occasion was 0–4–2T No. 532, one of the regular station pilots. Those old 0–4–2Ts were lovely little engines, simple to operate, with everything on them working like a watch and they would shunt for ages on a few shovels of coal.

We soon backed on to the train of some four or five four-wheel coaches and set off for Highworth. But the main thing I remember of the journey itself, except a feeling of bliss, was the fireman having to get down near Stanton station, open a level crossing gate, and close it again after we had passed through. What great days they were, especially the charm of a Great Western branch line as seen from the footplate. However, I blotted my copybook on return to Swindon station. The fireman went off for a can of tea and the driver got down to uncouple the train, leaving me alone on 532's footplate. Soon a voice from below shouted 'Ease up!' The coupling was too tight and the driver was calling for me to open the regulator gently to ease the engine towards the carriages and free the coupling. I was panic stricken; it flashed through my mind that if I opened the regulator I might injure or even kill the driver, or push the carriages backwards, so I did nothing. After a couple of similar calls, the driver came out from between the engine and coaches, climbed up the footplate and did the job himself having, of course, to get back down again and uncouple. During that couple of minutes, I got the full blast of unofficial railway vocabulary. . . .

In retrospect I wonder how many rules were broken that day, but a blind eye was certainly turned to the many footplate rides given to youngsters in the very heart of Swindon officialdom.

The strain of this occasion must have been too much for old 532, which had started life in 1868, as it was taken out of service only a few months afterwards. The other regular 0–4–2T pilots at the time were Nos. 217, 529, 539, 549, 551, 835, 837, 1158, 1436 and 1477. Besides shunting in the station area, some were in daily use as carriage shop pilots, whilst others had temporary spells at local branch line sheds such as Malmesbury or Faringdon, or occasionally at Chippenham.

From the hotel previously mentioned, the Whitehouse Road headed northwards, first passing under a long bridge which carried the main line, relief lines and associated sidings, then passing in rapid succession under four smaller bridges which carried sidings to carriage and wagon repair shops. Normally there was little to interest the enthusiast in what passed over those bridges, but we used to go and look up at the first of the four of them just before six o'clock in the evening, when a long line of repaired wagon stock was taken away from the shop sidings to return to traffic. It was not so much the wagons we went to see, but the four or five mineral brake vans that were regularly included. Often these were from constituent lines and carried (to us at least) such romantic-sounding names as Bassaleg, Rhymney (RR), Senghenydd, Cardiff, Cathays, Duffryn Yard, Machynlleth and Aberystwyth. We enjoyed trying to pronounce these difficult names; I know now that the result was far different to the smooth, somewhat musical, way I hear them pronounced now that I live in Wales.

The principal carriage and wagon works shunters were six small outside-cylinder short-wheelbase 0-6-0 saddle tanks, Nos. 1394–1399. These had originated on the Cornwall Minerals Railway and had been built in 1873. Despite the fact that they seemed absolutely dwarfed when moving modern G.W. carriages, they did a lot of hard work and seemed excellent engines for the job. Doubtless they had been chosen because of the sharp curves in some of the wagon sidings. As far as I recollect, all except 1398 had open-backed cabs, but that one had an overall roof to the small bunker.

There were also a number of small G.W. inside-cylinder 0-6-0 pannier tanks on similar works and those I recall in the 1926/7 period were Nos. 94, 868, 869, 994, 1928, 1933 (saddle tank), 1934, 2012, 2015 and 2017. I remember No. 1928 particularly well, as it was the regular Timber Yard pilot at The Boards, and frequently obstructed my view of the main line by depositing wagons in the way. During the summer of 1927 I used to think it would be quite a coincidence if engine 1928 would be shunting The Boards during 1928, but it was not to be, as it went into factory in November and was transferred to Cardiff East Dock on release. Although its replacement, No. 2014, worked The Boards for a while, it soon ceased to be a one-engine job as it had been with the 1928.

Down at the loco works the pilots were invariably standard 0-6-0 pannier tanks, usually the older types with outside frames. Thus it was a great surprise when No. 28 Cleobury became the East End pilot in 1931. This was an 0-6-0 saddle tank with outside cylinders from the Cleobury, Mortimer & Ditton Priors Railway, a company with a long title but only two engines. No. 28 stayed on the job for possibly three or four months, but finally went into shops where it was rebuilt as a pannier tank, losing its nameplate in the process. Both the A Shop and East End pilots were always engines sent to Swindon for repair, and were used for a while before going into factory or, more often, to the scrap yard. Neither were allocated to Swindon shed, as were the carriage and wagon works pilots, and each was stabled and serviced in its 'own' yard, the East End pilot in the works main reception sidings, and the other in the A Shop yard.

The smaller tank engines had their post-repair trial runs on the through sidings between the two yards mentioned, running up and down the half a mile under varying conditions – full speed, slow speed, blower on, cylinder cocks and brake tests etc., until the trial inspector was satisfied or had completed his routine examinations. Naturally a lot of weird sounds were heard from the engines during those trial runs, and one I particularly recall, late in 1927 or early in 1928, was by Wantage tram engine No. 7, a tiny Manning Wardle 0–4–0ST. On the tramway it leisurely ambled its way along the roadside from Wantage Town to Wantage Road station, or vice versa and rarely, one imagines, at anything faster than a brisk trot. On the trial road at Swindon, with the regular full open, it thundered along the track with exhaust barking loudly in protest, and with smoke shooting out from its tall narrow chimney. Probably it was not actually moving at much above 25 m.p.h., but with such a small loco, pushed to the limit it seemed very much faster. Both Wantage tram engines paid regular visits to Swindon factory, for light and heavy repairs, and were dealt with in the B Shed.

Returning to the station area, one engine I shall always associate with the Whitehouse was 4–6–0 2971 *Albion*. This was a Swindon engine for a long time, and usually shedded at Bristol during the periods it escaped from headquarters. I must have seen it hundreds of times between 1927 and 1936, during which period it frequently brought in a train that terminated at Swindon, and which it had to back on to the down carriage sidings previously mentioned. To do this it had to pass on the near side of the Station East Signalbox, where normally only the pilot shunted or simmered during quiet spells. Apart from its nameplate, *Albion* was a standard 29xx of the earlier batches with straight footplating under the cab sides, leaving a very high footstep to mount to get into the cab. However, its main attractions were the delightful nameplates which, although having the normal size letters and brass beading, were only about half the length of standard nameplates, where wide spacing was left on each side to accommodate short names. With *Albion* each plate was curved around immediately before and after the lettering, thus making it so short. Another variation was there was no distance plate below the lettered section; it was so short and light that it was fitted directly on the splasher. My friend Haydn Robinson, who shared that downpour with me on The Dump on Bonfire Night 1927, is now the proud owner of one of *Albion's* plates.

However, the main attraction at the station was the daily departure of the Cheltenham Flyer, weekends excluded. This train was gradually speeded up, and in 1932, was attracting world-wide attention by its regular non-stop runs between Swindon and Paddington, being at that time allowed 67 minutes for the 77,25 miles. This was easily the fastest booked run in the British Isles at the time. Actually we somewhat resented the name Cheltenham, as it was a stopping train (Gloucester, Stroud and Kemble) between that place and Swindon; the high-speed running came only after leaving Swindon. But what matter, it was the G.W.R. that counted, proving its superiority once again. Whilst any Castle from Old Oak Common worked the train, there were two regulars that seemed to be involved whenever anything beyond the normal was expected, namely 5000 *Launceston Castle* and 5006 *Tregenna Castle*.

The train ran into the Up Gloucester platform at Swindon just before a quarter to four, and there was always an air of occasion as it approached. Every day the Castle with its seven carriages would be met by a bowler-hatted loco inspector complete with flower in buttonhole. He was waiting where the engine pulled up, and had a cheery word with the driver to ensure all was well. At precisely 3.48 p.m. the green flag was waved and everyone in the vicinity stopped to watch the magic of a Castle in peak condition start its run to Paddington. No hesitation, no slipping, it was out of the platform like a shot out of a gun. I never saw anything like it afterwards until some similar starts from rest by the HST in recent years. The loud exhaust bark of the first few revolutions was quickly silenced as the driver reversed to 'cut-off' as the engine was leaving the platform, winding the screw reverse with one hand as he waved farewell to the inspector with the other. He knew, and everyone else knew that, barring miracles, he would have a clear path to Paddington, would reach 60 m.p.h. in three miles and 80 in six miles, remaining at around that speed until the outskirts of London. What a train, and what a wonderful daily performance, not a once-only specially prepared run.

Almost thirty-three years later, on 21 January 1965, I was waiting for a train on the main up platform at Cardiff General station on a bitterly cold morning, listening to the announcer repeating that 'B.R. regrets' that such-and-such train was running late. In the gloom, 2–8–0 3812 slowly passed down the centre road hauling two dead, and dirty, steam engines towards the scrap yard at Morriston, Swansea. One of them was none other than my old friend *Launceston Castle*, but now stripped of both name and number plates. No-one else even glanced at the rusting pair heading westwards. I smiled somewhat sadly as I thought of that same engine and her magnificent feats on the Flyer from 1929 onwards. Nevertheless the thought warmed me up as my mind's eye recalled the scenes in 1932, when I often witnessed this same engine setting out from Swindon like a thoroughbred in perfect condition with that confident look on the driver's face that he would be in Paddington not just on time, but a minute or two early. They were memories that could not be erased by the chill winds and the inexcusable 'B.R. regrets'.

The other daily spectacular, at least to me, was the appearance of an L.N.E.R. engine and its train. This arrived during the night, after which the engine was berthed in Swindon shed, while the crew adjourned to a house in Farnsby Street, where they enjoyed 'bed and supper' before their return to Sheffield late evening. The engine left shed about 8.30 p.m. and ambled leisurely on the up loco road to the station. On getting the 'board', it went on to the sidings to the east, then reversed and backed on to the three or four L.N.E.R. carriages berthed in the up bay (usually No. 6). Shortly afterwards a train from the west came into the main up platform where it divided, the Star class continuing with the front section to Paddington. The L.N.E.R. engine then pulled out of the bay with its short train and backed on to the rear half of the other train, and, at 9.05 p.m. precisely set off on the long journey northwards via Oxford and Banbury.

The first time I saw this train would be about 1926/7 and the engine was former Great Northern Atlantic No. 4428. This class remained on the duty for several years. The train was not always worked by the L.N.E.R.; after several months the G.W. would take over, and then again it would revert to the L.N.E.R. after a spell. In this manner the train worked at least until B.R. days, and probably much later. During the 1927–30 period, I saw various Atlantics on this run, including Nos. 3276, 3277, 3295, 4428, 4433, 4434 and 4449. All those were frequent visitors. By regularly going to the station to look at the L.N.E.R. engine at close range, I became a familiar figure there and one of the drivers took pity on the poor lad standing there watching trains. As a result, I was allowed up on the footplate. This was not only whilst the engine stood in the bay, but also during the movement between platforms. What a delightful experience that was. The Atlantics were kept spotlessly clean, and doubtless the Sheffield shed foreman only sent engines in peak condition out on this duty, to the very heart of the G.W.R.

The timings at week-ends were entirely different, and we were able to see two L.N.E.R. engines within an hour early on Sunday afternoons. The train which had arrived about two o'clock on Saturday morning did not leave again until about three p.m. on Sunday, whilst the train which left Swindon at 9.05 on Friday evening returned about 2 p.m. on Sunday afternoon, hence on Sunday afternoons the one L.N.E.R. engine arrived at Swindon shed as the other was leaving.

Only once during the first few years did I see any other engine on that job apart from the ex-G.N. Atlantics, and that was another Atlantic, painted black, from the former Great Central carrying L.N.E.R. No. 6094. This was probably on a Sunday afternoon in 1931, but I did not make a note of the date, and I never saw another G.C. Atlantic on the turn. However, about 1933 the G.N. Atlantics disappeared for a while and G.C. 4-4-0 inside-cylinder Directors took their place. Three were regulars, 5437 *Prince George*, 5501 *Mons* and 5502 *Zeebrugge*, all, if my memory is correct, painted black. Although I did not see the train so often afterwards, by 1935/6 the G.N. Atlantics were again quite frequently on the turn until 1937 when 4-6-0s of the Sandringham class took over. 2863 *Everton*, 2864 *Liverpool* and 2865 *Leicester City* were the regulars, although a G.N. Atlantic still put in an occasional appearance. I left Swindon in 1938 and after the war I only saw the L.N.E.R. train occasionally on Sunday afternoons, when the engines were B1 4-6-0s.

Of the G.W. engines seen regularly at the station, I remember the Bulldogs best, as they were one of my favourite classes. Regulars were 3319 *Weymouth*, 3326 *Laira*, 3329 *Mars*, 3340 *Camel*, 3341 *Blasius*, 3373 *Sir William Henry*, 3375 *Sir Watkin Wynn*, 3379 *River Fal*, 3430 *Inchcape* and 3451 *Pelican*. Most of these had a spell at Swindon shed in the 1927-31 period, or were at nearby sheds and visited us regularly, mainly on stopping trains from Gloucester, Westbury, Reading and sometimes Bristol. There was one duty we looked forward to each morning, and that was an arrival from Gloucester just after ten o'clock. The Bulldog came off this train and went back to shed; if no down train obstructed the view, we caught a brief glimpse of it passing the Whitehouse before reversing on to the shed road. If we did miss it, we had a second chance by going on the platform, as it returned on a Gloucester 'stopper' about 11.15. Our special interest in this particular Bulldog was that it was not worked by a Gloucester one, but usually a 'scarce' one that had worked through from Hereford.

Mention has already been made of some of the Saint class seen regularly at Swindon, such as *Albion* and those on the South Wales expresses in the early period. Other regulars of the early period on less strenuous duties were 2923 *Saint George*, 2942 *Fawley Court* and, later, 2927 *Saint Patrick*, 2935 *Caynham Court*, 2939 *Croome Court*, 2953 *Titley Court* and 2954 *Tockenham Court*. Most had spells at Swindon shed, although few of the class were really scarce, as they worked in from all parts of the G.W. system.

Of the goods engines, the two that I recall best were 2–8–0s Nos. 2807 and 2872, which for most of 1928 and 1929 worked overnight between Swindon and Newton Abbot and vice versa. They were double home turns, the engines working from the Swindon end on alternate evenings. No. 2807 was a Newton Abbot engine and 2872 was at Swindon. The goods left Swindon about 8.30 p.m. and was a long heavy train; I often saw it leave and thought of the long night ahead for the crew. Both engines were called into factory early in 1930, and on release transferred to St. Phillips Marsh shed at Bristol. It is pleasing to note that 2807 has recently been rescued, for preservation, from Woodham's yard at Barry, where it had been rusting peacefully away for nearly eighteen years.

An oddity to be seen at the station was the old steam rail cars. One of these used to leave just after 2.00 p.m. for Chippenham, and I often went to look at it in No. 3 down bay prior to departure. They were odd-looking vehicles with a large vertical boiler enclosed within the carriage and a small chimney sticking out above the roof. It usually had an eight-wheel clerestory carriage as a trailer – and obviously objected to it, as whenever I saw it from one of my regular spots at the west end of town, I could hear it coming from when it was just clear of the station. It huffed, puffed and snorted, and generally created so much fuss and clatter that I was surprised any such cars still existed. There is no doubt, though, that they had been a successful cost-cutting exercise for the G.W.R. in the early years of the century, before they had been generally replaced by push-and-pull trains. The steam cars ceased to work in the Swindon area about 1930 or 1931.

A number of local trains were recognised running-in turns for engines ex-factory. For passenger engines, these would usually be to Bristol, Reading or Didcot and back. The larger tank engines would also take a turn to Didcot, also the early evening workmen's train to Kemble. One evening I was up in the cab of 4–4–2 County tank No. 2243, on its first turn out of the factory, when the driver asked if I would like a ride to Kemble and back. Naturally enough I would, and what impressed me was the large roomy cab compared to the 0–4–2T pilots that I was more used to riding on. However, there was a massive reversing lever, and the one on 2243 was stiff after its spell in factory, and I recall the driver heaving, sweating and tugging as he swore at some unknown fitter who had assembled it. Apart from that it was a very pleasant trip, the train resting at Kemble for fifty minutes before returning to Swindon as a local passenger train.

# 7

## *Round and About, 1930s*

WHILST STANDING AT THE Whitehouse, we would sometimes get rest-less and go for a walk 'under the bridges', turning left into Ferndale Road from where we could walk to the bottom of Rodbourne Road and return under the main line to Park Lane, close to both The Boards and the churchyard. On the south side of Ferndale Road was another recreation ground (Ferndale Rec.) which bordered the embankment to No. 24 Shop, one of the new carriage workshops. Outside the shop at the north-east corner stood an 0–6–0 saddle tank, without number plates, that was used as a stationary boiler. It had a long stovepipe extension to the chimney and a steam feed pipe from the top of the dome. Without an engine number, we only took a passing interest in it, despite rumours that it had once belonged to the old Briston & Exeter Railway. I found out at a later date that it had indeed been B. & E. No. 77, built in 1867 and condemned as G.W.R. No. 1360 in 1890. After that date it worked as a stationary boiler at different places, and was put down outside No. 24 Shop in 1927, where it lasted until scrapped in 1944.

Another oddity was an outside-framed inside-cylinder 2–4–0 sad-dle tank with a long straight chimney, which was stored in the Spare Machinery Stores, not far from the back of the Points and Crossings Shop. We used to call that Stores the Crystal Palace, as it had a large curved roof which contained glass sections to increase the light in-side, the rest being made of steel corrugated sheeting. Inside the stores were all manner of items or machinery, and on one side a pile of numberplates from 7322 upwards. These had been cast for further 2–6–0s which in the event were never built. Also, of course, there was the little engine standing on its own wheels. This had originally been a South Devon Railway broad gauge engine named *Prince*, built in 1871 and converted to standard gauge in 1893. Six years later it had been altered for stationary work and, as such, lasted until September 1933, although it was always a spare in the Crystal Palace in my day. Afterwards it was pushed down The Dump and cut up there in August 1935.

The Dump seemed to get plenty of oddities in the late 1920s and 1930s. Another broad gauge relic had turned up there in 1929. This was *Hedley*, which had started life as a 2–4–0 passenger engine in 1865. Twelve years later it was altered to a saddle tank and lasted out the broad gauge as such. After 1892 it was put to stationary boiler work, spending most of its days at Neath District Civil Engineers' Depot. Apart from wheels it was still complete, even to nameplates, when I saw it on The Dump in the summer of 1929.

Late in 1932 a narrow gauge engine arrived there, one of the Vale of Rheidol 2–6–2Ts, No. 1212. As was the case with a lot of absorbed engines taken out of service at the time, it was placed on the Sales List, and remained on the Dump until cut up in March 1935. During that year the four G.W.R. crane engines arrived on The Dump. Three had been purpose-built at Swindon, Nos. 16 *Hercules*, 17 *Cyclops* and 18 *Steropes*, whilst the fourth was another former South Devon Railway 2–4–0 side tank, No. 1299, which had been fitted in 1881 with a crane of 1½-tons lifting capacity. No. 17 always worked at Stafford Road factory in Wolverhampton, the other three at Swindon, being always stabled outside the east end of that section of B Shed that originally had been the broad gauge engine shed, where I could see them when settled on the fence at the back of the churchyard. During the demolition of that part of the B Shed late in 1929, the crane engines were temporarily moved elsewhere, probably to the works sidings on the west side of the Gloucester line, but returned to their former haunt once the rubble had been cleared.

The three Swindon-built engines had jibs which rested in the lowered position when not in use, but that on No. 1299 was fixed in the upright position and could only swivel horizontally. Although I regularly saw them pottering around the works sidings in the 1925–32 period, I never recall seeing one actually lift a load. They frequently disappeared down the Dump sidings, and presumably they were used lifting scrap into wagons, as well as in the adjacent Timber Yard area of the Saw Mills. After the new engine and boiler scrapping shop opened in 1932, they seemed to be little used, although on occasion they were borrowed by the Civil Engineering Dept. for various jobs, particularly at week-ends.

I first saw *Cyclops* on 18 December 1933 when it arrived in the A Shop yard from Stafford Road, its work there having finished, presumably due to the rebuilding of that factory. Whilst it reposed in the yard month in and month out, in sunshine and rain, the other three were 'Stopped' (to see them there daily at that period, you would never know they had started) and were transferred to one of the dead-end sidings alongside the iron foundry. On 12 February 1935 No. 17 was moved down to the Dump sidings where Nos. 16, 18 and 1299 also arrived soon afterwards. Down there they had one brief spell of glory as cinema newsreel cameras went there and took shots of them; this film was shown, sandwiched between the two main films, as a news item under the title of 'The Locomotive Graveyard'. They were finally cut up early in 1938, No. 16 in January, No. 17 in February and the other two in March.

Long before that date, The Dump itself had changed dramatically. The old loco. sidings (Nos. 4 to 18) had filled up in 1928 with the withdrawal of many standard G.W. types − 4−4−0s of the City and Flower classes, a large number of 0−6−0 saddle and pannier tanks, 0−4−2 side tanks, plus the R.O.D.s earmarked for early withdrawal, plus still more constituent engines replaced by standard G.W. classes. Still on hand at the start of that year were most of the engines put on the Sales List in October 1926 and subsequently, hence a speed-up in cutting up was vital, or the sidings would be full. Initially the Sales List engines were taken off the list and cut up, but this took most of the latter half of 1928 and early 1929 as normal cutting-up had to be maintained as far as possible. The position became acute again in 1930 and 1931 when further G.W. classes were withdrawn, such as the 4−4−0 Counties, the 4−4−2 County tanks, the 3600 class 2−4−2Ts and 3900 class 2−6−2Ts − those long side tank engines with the huge 'hole' near the bottom of the tanks for ease of servicing. On top of those extra classes, dozens of the old 0−4−2 and 0−6−0 tanks were being withdrawn as they were replaced by new construction. It seemed that all the fleet of engines I knew, and loved, in 1927 were being wiped out.

It was obvious that the old method of breaking up engines in the open could not cope, so a new cutting-up workshop was erected towards the close of 1932 at the north-west corner of the Dump site, not far from the old cutting-up line. No date was announced for the opening of the new C Shop, but it was probably early in December 1932, as in the diaries of Phil Reed is an entry covering one of his

Swindon visits, dated 11 December 1932 –

On old scrap siding – Nos. 648 and 744 (both 0–6–0Ts).

In new scrap shed – Nos. 534, 553, 839, 1018, 1736 and 3906 (three 0–4–2Ts, two 0–6–0Ts and one 2–6–2T).

The sidings around the shop had to be completely re-arranged and the old scrap sidings soon disappeared, to be replaced by two long sidings on which to store engines awaiting scrap. The old storage sidings (Nos. 4 to 18) were full at the time, but cutting-up was much more rapid in the new shop where it was not affected by the weather, and where there was an overhead crane, plate cutting machines and ample oxy-acetylene burning gear available. Despite a further mass withdrawal of fifty engines on 2 July 1932 (of which fourteen were added to the once again growing Sales List) the old sidings soon thinned out and, apart from wagon stock, only housed engines on the Sales List afterwards. It was difficult to understand why some of the engines had been put on the list, as there was little hope of buyers for –

| No. | | | Condemned | Cut-up |
|-----|-----|-----|-----------|--------|
| 919 | Old T.V.R. | 0–6–0 tender engine | 22/2/1930 | 10/3/1934 |
| 1110 | Cambrian | 4–4–0 tender engine | 18/4/1931 | 7/4/1934 |
| 1319 | Barry | 2–4–2T | 7/3/1930 | 30/7/1932 |
| 3505 | G.W. | 2–4–0 tender engine | 18/4/1931 | 9/2/1935 |
| 4150 | *Begonia* | 4–4–0 tender engine | 18/4/1931 | 7/4/1934 |

Besides these, there were also 4113 *Samson* and the Vale of Rheidol 2–6–2T No. 1212 already mentioned.

Not finding buyers, those six standard gauge engines worked their way down the sidings to the buffer stops where I could see them from the Wootton Bassett Road. Of the more saleable engines, those I remember best were four Taff Vale 0–6–2 side tanks, Nos. 502, 552, 581 and 593. These were all condemned in August 1930 and put on The Dump sidings, but they must have attracted a lot of enquiries, as the East End pilot was regularly occupied going down there and returning with two of them – usually 502 and 593. Presumably they were inspected by prospective buyers, as, after an hour or two, they would be pushed back down again. Only 581 was sold, in 1932, the others being cut up in 1934.

There were also two small 0–4–0ST dock engines on the Sales List, Nos. 1339 (Cardiff Railway) and 1340 *Trojan* (Alexandra Docks and Railway, Newport). So far as is known, they were never put on The Dump, being stored on the sidings in front of the iron foundry, and later on one of the traverser table roads between B Shed and the foundry. No. 1339 was taken out of service in May 1932 and finally cut up at the end of June 1934. *Trojan*, which reached Swindon on 26 July 1932, was just saved from scrapping by being sold (for £90) in the same month it was due to be scrapped with 1339. Happily, *Trojan* is still with us at Didcot, her name or numberplates now being worth many times more than the whole engine was sold for in 1934!

It was probably in 1935, or soon afterwards, that the old Dump sidings stabled their last engines; once the unsold engines had been broken up, engines added to the withdrawal list were stabled on the new sidings adjacent to the C Shop, and the old sidings full of engines as I knew them so well in the late 1920s were turned over to wagon storage only. Before leaving the subject of them though there is one amusing incident that happened in the summer of 1931 worth recounting. From the Wootton Bassett Road a County class 4–4–0 was visible next but one to the stop blocks, but I could not see either the name or numberplate. One day when I was there a workman walked along the path at the top of the embankment, so I called up and asked if he would mind walking up the sidings and letting me know the name of the engine. He was gone several minutes and I assumed he had not bothered, when suddenly he reappeared. He had the nameplate over his shoulder, which he turned so that I could read *County of Cornwall*, and then walked off! By sheer coincidence, he had evidently been sent to recover the plate and take it to the Stores!

Some larger engines, 4–6–0s of the Saint and Star classes, were cut up in the C Shop in the 1930s, but it was usual in those cases for the engine to go into the A Shop first. Here the boiler was taken out of the frame, and doubtless repaired and used again. The strange-looking assembly of frame, wheels and cabside was then dispatched to The Dump, looking most odd with the large vertical copper injector pipes, so familiar in the cab of an engine, hanging loose between the cab sides. Twenty Aberdare 2–6–0s were similarly treated when they were taken out of service, nominally in lieu of 'new' 2–8–2Ts of the 7200 class in 1934, and during the Autumn of that year you could always see a few Aberdares standing without their boilers in the A Shop yard and on The Dump. In connection with the engines the Accountants performed the feat of disposing of two engines for each new (converted) engine added. No. 7200 was a conversion from 2–8–0T 5275, but in the Accountants' books it also replaced Aberdare 2602. So 5275 and 2602 were taken out of the book stock, but only one engine, No. 7200, added. . . .

The Accountants made some other strange decisions, at least to railway enthusiasts, in the period under review. In 1925/6 a number of constituent engines were sent to private locomotive firms for

*One of Swindon's regular station pilots from 1923 until condemned in 1935 was 0–4–2T No. 835, photographed here outside the loco shed in 1928.*

*[Author's Collection]*

*Former South Devon Railway 2–4–0ST 'Prince' in the Spare Machinery Stores destined for use as a stationary boiler, circa 1930.*

*[Lens of Sutton]*

Wantage Tram 0–4–0ST No.7 and No.6003 'King George IV' posed in the A Shop yard on 1 November 1927. Note the Barn visible in the background.

[British Railways]

complete overhaul and, despite returning in much the same external condition, these were nominally condemned, and then put back into stock on their return. Their mileage records even started all over again as 'new' engines. On the other hand identical engines which had been overhauled at Swindon, including those completely rebuilt with G.W. standard boilers, cabs, bunkers etc were neither taken out of stock in the same manner, nor were their mileages affected.

In 1936 6007 *King William III* was condemned by the Accountants after the tragic Shrivenham smash on 15 January. A 'replacement' 6007 was put into traffic on 24 March. In fact the engine, boiler and tender were repaired, and no new engine was constructed. I watched the progress of that repair, seeing it most days, and the boiler never even came out of the frame. I suppose that, as the heavy out-of-course repair costs had to be booked to something, a Swindon Lot No. was issued, which led many enthusiasts to believe that an entirely new engine had been constructed.

Before leaving The Dump – which was the topic before one thing led to another – I would mention that in the late 1920s it appeared to be on fire when seen from the West End Rec. at night. In the darkness there were two or three areas glowing red, although in the daytime you could see no signs of fire, no smoke or any particular heat. The Dump was on made-up ground, some fifteen feet high, which appeared to consist mostly of coke-type clinkers. At the time we took it to be spontaneous combustion. I never did hear whether it was put out, or burned itself out, but something must have happened as, fifty years later (in 1981) the site is still there, despite the sidings having been taken up about four years ago.

I suppose that, between the Wars, Trip Week was the most eagerly looked forward-to event in the Swindon calendar. That was the annual mass exodus of the works' employees and their families to the seaside. Although there was no such thing as paid holidays at the time, apart from salaried staff, 'Trip' was the principal topic of all and sundry for weeks ahead. The G.W.R. provided the trains free of charge, and normally arranged the event in late June/early July so as not to clash with the main holiday season, hence Swindon schools had their summer holidays a few weeks earlier than normal elsewhere. The holiday itself actually started and terminated on Fridays, the giant railway works being closed from lunch time on Thursday to the following Monday week.

For weeks beforehand the shops in the town, particularly clothing shops, did a roaring trade as new suits, blazers, flannel trousers, frocks and blouses were purchased in readiness, as were swimming costumes, beach balls, buckets, spades and the like. Eventually all was set for the great day, which virtually turned Swindon into a ghost town. The population at the time was somewhere above 50,000 and out of those the best part of 28,000 would travel on the holiday specials. These were all timed to leave between about 5 o'clock and 8 o'clock on the Friday morning, except some four or five long-distance trains which left late Thursday evening for St. Ives, Penzance and the Cambrian coast.

Sufficient people always went to St. Ives to warrant running two trains, and on the occasion I travelled in one we went non-stop to Newton Abbot where, at about two in the morning, there was a lengthy stop for toilet and refreshment purposes. It was quite novel to see the platform refreshment trollies out in force, sustaining people, at that hour of the morning. Then on to St. Erth non-stop, where a couple of 2–6–2Ts of the 4400 or early 4500 series were waiting to back on to the train and take it over the short branch to St. Ives. Without exaggeration, nearly half of the population of that delightful Cornish holiday resort were at the station to welcome the Swindon trains, at six o'clock in the morning! (The fact that the better class of visitor, also the well-known artists, gave St. Ives a wide berth during Trip Week need not be enlarged upon here). The St. Ives-Swindon week was really something in those days. Special charabanc and boating trips would be arranged, additional services in the church, various sports fixtures between the two towns arranged. The local lasses who worked at the silk factory always welcomed the Swindon lads, and even the lifeboat was specially launched for the benefit of the Swindon visitors who, undoubtedly, spent a lot of money in the Cornish resort during the week.

After the overnight trains had left Swindon (these all left from the station) all was quiet for a few hours before the great exodus began. Long before four in the morning houses were alive with lights, and within an hour the excited chatter of children could be heard all over the town as people began making their way towards the works, as it was from various works' sidings that the majority of the early morning trains departed. Despite special trams being run to get the trippers to the works, plus cabs and taxis working to capacity, the majority still had to walk, due to the huge numbers involved. Even at that early hour, shops selling newspapers, cigarettes, sweets, cups of tea, buns and sandwiches were open and doing great business. Many westbound trains started from the Carriage and Wagon sidings on the south side of the line, between Park Lane and the carriage shops near the station, where at least four trains could be stabled at one time. Wooden steps were placed against the carriage footboards to enable the mass of bodies, suitcases, bags, and buckets and spades to get into the trains.

Those sidings were principally used for Weymouth and Weston-super-Mare (five or six trains to each) and Barry Island (two trains), plus single trains to one or two other western resorts. On one occasion I travelled to Barry Island behind a 4300 class 2–6–0, and we ran direct from the siding to Barry Island station non-stop. It seemed strange to pass through the large stations at Newport and Cardiff without stopping.

Another popular destination was Paddington, for which about six trains left, most from the up sidings in front of the C.M. & E.E.s offices, but one or two from the station. The people on those trains were only passing through London of course, changing to another line in the Capital to complete their journey. One train that did go through to 'foreign' metals, as other railways were then called, was the most exciting to all the enthusiasts, as it comprised a Southern Railway engine and rolling stock. This was the Trip train to Portsmouth and Southsea, and we were always down at Barnes' yard about eight o'clock on the Thursday evening to see the empty stock arrive. It came over the M.S.W.J. line from Andover Junction, and always comprised a L.S.W.R. 4–4–0 of the T9 Class with a rake of L.S.W.R. bogie carriages. The strange thing about it, apart from seeing a complete Southern train at Swindon, was that the engine was always tender-first as it passed around the loop through Rushey Platt to the main line, the eight-wheel tender intriguing us, as the only one on the G.W. at that time was the one originally coupled to *The Great Bear*. I never did find out why it arrived tender-first, or where the engine was turned – probably the latter was carried out at Old Town station to relieve the pressure at Swindon shed on their busiest night of the year, although the engine must have been stabled there prior to its early morning departure.

All told, about 30–32 trains carried the trippers away, all but the few long distance overnight trains departing within three hours in the early morning. It was a marvellous feat of organisation, starting with the issue of application forms for tickets some two or three months beforehand, arranging the timetable of special trains to suit the various choices of resort, borrowing locomotives and carriages from various depots, clearing the works sidings needed for the trains, plus the stabling and departure of the trains themselves, but everything always seemed to go smoothly; moreover, normal train services were not interrupted. During Trip Week, Swindon was virtually dead and many small businesses closed for the week, but Trip Wednesday was the quietest day of all. That was the normal early closing day, and the opportunity was taken by most of the large shops to close for the whole day, enabling the staffs to take a day outing themselves.

On the following Friday, the Trip trains returned from the various resorts, arriving throughout the evening at Swindon station, and not the sidings. Thousands of suntanned Swindonians, with open-necked shirts in their sports jackets and fancy blouses, returned with their bulging cases and still chattering children, and made their way home, the Trip over for another year. Alas, Trip Week at Swindon is now a thing of the past, but for those who knew, and participated in that excitement in pre-war days, it was an event never to be forgotten.

# 8

## *The GWR and its town of Swindon*

THE TOWNSFOLK OF Swindon enjoyed many other benefits through the breadwinners' employment at the Works. The G.W.R. Medical Fund, as it was called, was by far the most important. Commencing in 1847 this met the medical needs of Swindon Works' employees, as well of all members of their families, literally from the cradle to the grave. It was far and away in advance of anything similar at the time, and became the model on which the National Health Service was later based.

The main Medical Centre was part of a large building at the corner of Faringdon Road and Milton Road, close to the present G.W.R. Railway Museum. It was laid out, all those years ago, in a better way than many Health Centres today. The ground floor comprised a large area with seven or eight doctors' consulting rooms down two sides, with two rows of seats facing each other, with a wide space between for each surgery. The remainder of the floor was occupied by a large dispensary with several serving hatches; there was also a small office where, after nominating the doctor of your choice, you received a brass disc with a number on it. Outside each doctor's room was a small box with a glass window which contained a reel of numbers, which each patient moved on as he went into the room. Thus you knew exactly how many were in front of you and, if you wished, you could go outside shopping or what you will, until you estimated your turn was approaching. The system worked perfectly, no booking days in advance, and as you left the surgery the dispensary attended to your needs straight away. Each patient had an individual medical book in which the doctor entered any prescription, although for minor items the book could be presented at the dispensary without having to see a doctor.

If further treatment was required, the doctor sent you up to the next floor where there was a dental surgery, an ear nose and throat department, an ophthalmic department, together with physiotherapists and a chiropodist. If specialist treatment was required, there were arrangements with certain London and other major hospitals to which you were sent. Just across the road from this pioneer Health Centre was the G.W.R. Hospital and a separate large outpatients' department. All that for just a few pence per week. The remainder of the Medical Fund block was taken up by two indoor swimming pools, which used to be boarded over for meetings and dances during the winter months, whilst there were also washing and turkish baths. Few of the houses in Swindon had baths in those days, of course.

The G.W.R. had a hand in almost everything connected with the well-being of their Swindon employees. Apart from being instrumental in setting up St. Marks Church, as already mentioned, they also provided a large park alongside. Before my time cricket matches were held on the Park, and I remember my grandfather saying that the immortal W. G. Grace once played there. The pavilion was still there when I was a lad, although it was then derelict with the floor boards creaking and doors blowing back and forth with the wind. On the other side of the Park was a bandstand where, on occasions, we were treated to a brass band recital. As it had long since become a public park in my young days, the G.W.R. handed it over to the local authority in 1925, in exchange for some land to build a further carriage workshop on the north side of town. I well remember the fêtes that used to be held in the Park. That amusing railway historian and author, A. H. Ahrons related that, at one time, a locomotive tender would be cleaned out, stabled on the siding at the top of Park Lane, and the water boiled in it to provide tea for the huge crowds at the fêtes. In my days it was not as exciting as that, but it was still a big day. The fêtes were opened, at 1.30 p.m. on a Saturday, by the firing of a cannon. We youngsters paid a 'Joey' (3d) to get in, and were given a greaseproof paper bag containing a huge slice of greasy, but delicious cake. With this was a ticket, stuck between the cake and the bag, for a free ride on a roundabout.

In 1931 the G.W.R. opened a modern sports ground off Shrivenham Road, on the eastern outskirts of town. This included a cricket ground, bowling greens, putting and tennis courts, plus provision for hockey and outdoor rifle practice. In the pavilion there were a bar, skittle alley, changing rooms and baths.

The company had also provided for education in the period before that was taken over by the county education authority, constructing a massive building, immediately opposite the main tunnel entrance to the works, known as the Mechanics Institute. At one time advanced students were taught there but in my day it comprised a library, and large reading room, billiards room and chess room, with a theatre on the top floor. I vividly recall the night of Christmas Eve 1930, when my Mother woke me up shouting, 'The Mechanics Institute is on fire!' Sure enough, across the Park, the sky was lit up by the flames of the burning building. It was like Trip morning again, lights on in all the houses and people, including myself, hurrying to the scene. Fortunately the building was not destroyed, in fact it stands today, but a completely new theatre had to be built. The other thing I remember about the Mechanics Institute was the large metal weathervane in the form of the *Lord of the Isles* broad gauge loco, which stood above the west corner tower, opposite the Tunnel Entrance. I spent many happy hours in the Reading Room there in the 1930s, as it contained all the railway journals of the day. Above the double swing doors entrance was mounted a nameplate from one of the old Dean singles, *Royal Sovereign*. It was the old type of plate, without brass beading, which I was not familiar with despite having seen 4170 *Charles Saunders*, 4171 *Armstrong* and 4172 *Gooch* still running with those type of plates until they were withdrawn 1928/9.

There were many other ways in which the G.W.R. looked after its workforce at Swindon. They had their own Savings Bank in London Street, which gave slightly higher interest rates than the main banks, and they provided house coal at greatly reduced rates, and also refuse timber. How well I remember the big cart horses, with G.W.R. horse brasses gleaming, slowly picking their way through the back lanes in New Town, delivering this coal every fortnight. It was our job, as youngsters, to follow them around with bucket and shovel, to advance the science of gardening.

One could almost fill a book with the benefits of being one of a railway family at Swindon in pre-war days; suffice to say that the G.W.R. really cared for its staff and their families. Doubtless that was what made Swindon such a close-knit community, and one that it is doubtful we shall see the like of again.

The company ensured that its workpeople started on time by providing the loudest hooter that I have ever heard. This was sounded several times a day, with either long, very long, or fairly short blasts which each had their separate meanings. The first went fairly early at seven o'clock in the morning, being a long blast to inform all and sundry that the working day had begun, and it was time to start getting ready. The next, a medium long blast, came at 7.50 to warn that there was just ten minutes to get to the workshop. Five minutes later there was a short blast which was called the warning hooter, signifying five minutes to go. You could see the masses of men on their way to work speed up as that hooter blew. Then came the eight o'clock hooter itself, which was a very long one, with the late comers scrambling to take their numbered brass time checks off the hooks on the check board before the sound stopped, as once it did the glass front on the check board was pulled down. Anyone who missed removing his check even by a few seconds had to wait for half an hour, after which the board would be re-opened, and a '½ hour' check put on the hook to replace the time check. Besides losing half an hour's pay, a second re-occurrence of this would usually mean a message to report to the office later, and explain.

There were no further blasts until 12.30, when work ceased. That was a long blast – although there was really no need, as everyone was ready. Then came the afternoon blasts, at 1.20, 1.25 and 1.30 for re-starting work, their lengths and meanings being the same as in the mornings. The main difference in this case was that if the glass front was pulled down on the check board before you had removed your check there was no half hour late second chance in the afternoon. Work and the hooter ceased for the day at 5.30 p.m., with another long final blast. There were thus nine blasts, all of which could be heard up to a dozen miles away if the wind was in the right direction, or about six miles away if not.

The Boiler House that produced this astounding sound had eight chimneys, each 120' high, each one constructed from the barrels of old locomotive boilers rivetted together. As this was situated only a quarter of a mile from where I lived, the residents at that west end of New Town got the full benefit of the hooter blasts. Other than the times mentioned, I only recall the hooter being sounded on two other occasions during the year. This was at 11 a.m. on Armistice Day, to mark the start and end of the two minutes silence during which time all work ceased at the factory, also in schools, shops and offices, plus all traffic in the streets. It also blew at midnight on New Year's Eve to welcome in the New Year. That was a particularly prolonged blast.

The sound of the hooter was a daily feature of the town; life was controlled by it, clocks and watches adjusted by it, and meals got out of the oven and dished up in readiness for the menfolk when it blew.

It was a small but important part of the life of the town.

Before leaving Swindon itself to describe some of my experiences working in the factory, I would mention that the company owned several streets of houses adjacent to the works in the Mechanics Institute area. These carried names of places served by the G.W.R., or on proposed routes in its early period, such as London, Reading, Oxford, Bathampton, Bristol, Taunton and Exeter. These terraced houses had been built in the infancy of the works, some adjoining houses having a common street entrance with front doors side by side, but at an angle to each other and leading directly into the respective living rooms. They were always referred to as 'The Company's Houses', as is still the case today. The grey stone exteriors were completely renovated in recent years after the houses were listed as of historic interest. The church and the park also came within the area of G.W.R. property and, in my young days, for one day each year a long wooden barrier was swung across the public roadway entrance to some of the streets, and locked in position to denote this private ownership. This did not affect the pavements which remained open to pedestrains. During the other 364 days of the year, the barrier was locked in position alongside the pavement.

Mention of the church reminds me of Radnor Street cemetery, up on the hill at the west end of town. From there a panoramic view of the works and sidings, from just west of the station to Rushey Platt Junction could be seen. It was from there that you realised just how many engines were actually in steam in the works area; there were puffs of smoke everywhere, which was white from the Welsh steam coal in use. The view made you realise the vastness of the railway works, and the immense area it occupied; it was difficult to visualise the situation ever changing.

At the locomotive works in the early 1930s, whilst there was plenty of interest on the scrapping side, new construction – rebuilding in many cases – added little to that interest. It was an era of replacement, with the smaller engines being replaced by very similar looking machines but with regimented numbers, whilst the old passenger engines we knew and loved were being replaced by numerous Halls and Castles with a monotonous series of names. No less than 120 Halls appeared between 1928 and 1931 and it soon became a joke in Swindon that the only one forgotten was *Henry Hall*, the leader of a popular dance orchestra at this time on the radio.

To make matters worse, many of the earlier names were being taken off engines on the flimsy excuse that some passengers thought they were going to whatever place name happened to be on the engine plate, such as *Reading, Cardiff* or *Taunton*. If so, there must have been some mild heart attacks when those with the names *Melbourne, Auckland, Quebec* or *Bombay* appeared at the front of those passengers' intended trains! It all seemed a rather tall story when names such as *Tregothnan, St. Columb* and *St. Aubyn* were taken off in 1930. In only one case was an attractive name substituted, *Pershore Plum* in place of *Plymouth* and that was, apparently, at the initiative of certain Worcestershire farmers.

As far as engine names were concerned on the G.W.R., there seemed to be a total lack of inspiration in the late 1920s and through the 1930s, not helped by the unholy mess made of naming the Bulldog/Duke rebuilds. It was originally intended that these should carry the name of the 'Duke' involved and the first, *St. Michael*, duly came out as such until someone hit on the idea of naming the engines after Earls. This neither cheered up the enthusiast or the nobility concerned, and the names had to be hastily removed and put on 'a better class of engine'. Their lordships felt honour was satisfied by this, whilst the enthusiast was glad that the never-ending succession of Castle class names had at last been broken. But it was said that the lovely old Duke names were not restored to the 3200 rebuilds.

It was not only engine names that had us saddened, for the changing of engine numbers was also a source of annoyance. This had started with the renumbering of certain 4300 and 5300s into a new 8300 series onwards for what seemed to be only a comparatively small alteration of weight at the front end (which in fact we did not then realise altered the loco's route availability). One could see the reason when 5200 series 2–8–0Ts were rebuilt as 2–8–2Ts and renumbered in the 7200 series. However, that was not the case with the 3100 class 2–6–2Ts which were renumbered in the 5100 series and some again, later, in the 8100 series, and why some of the 3150 class engines started being renumbered in the vacant 3100 group. It was all confusing at the time.

Perhaps even worse from the enthusiast's point of view was the addition of outside steam pipes to some of our beloved two-cylinder classes. We had accepted this with the four-cylinder Castles and Kings as they had been constructed with them but when, from the late 1920s onwards, engines came out of the A Shop with straight pipes, it seemed completely against the well-established G.W.R. principle of neat and tidily designed engines. No class was safe, tank or tender – the 2800s, the 4200s and the 4300s and the 4500s were all dealt with, and even my favourite Saints. However, even those seemed more acceptable than the queer inward-curving pipes fitted

*Swindon Junction station looking east, showing (left to right) the up main plat-
form, down main platform, down bays and down Gloucester platform.*

[Lens of Sutton]

*Crane engines 0–6–4T No. 16 'Hercules' and 2–4–0T No. 1299 stabled alongside
the B Shed, October 1931.* [P. J. T. Reed]

2–4–0 No.3217 was one of the 'Barnum' class, on which the author rode on its trial run to Brinkworth on 18 September 1933.

[Author's Collection]

to some of the Stars, which seemed uncertain whether they were intended as outside or inside steam admission pipes. Finally, the worst blow to our pride in G.W.R. locomotives was when 2935 *Caynham Court* was rebuilt at the works in May 1931 with rotary cam poppet valve gear and new cylinders. I can remember when I saw this Saint outside the A Shop, just out of factory, and thinking that was the last straw, and wondering why one of these graceful and beautiful 4–6–0s should be treated in this way. To make matters worse, it was shedded at Swindon more or less for the rest of its days, hence I had to endure the sight of it most days until I left Swindon seven years afterwards.

Even so, with all its faults, the G.W.R. was still supreme in my eyes, and, whilst I felt dismayed when William Stanier left Swindon in 1932 to take control of the locomotive department of the L.M.S., I did think that at least something worthwhile would now emerge from that quarter.

# 9

## *Apprenticeship, 1933–1938*

AFTER BEING AN ardent enthusiast for over eight years, my school days ended in the early summer of 1933, and I was apprenticed to fitting, turning and erecting in the Loco Works. This came as something of a shock to my family, as I came from a long line of coach bodybuilders going back to the stage coach era. My grandfather had moved down to Swindon from the Worcester area, his father having been with the old Oxford Worcester & Wolverhampton Railway. I first recollect him talking to me about railways in 1923 when he told me about the new carriages being built by his gang (he was a chargeman) for the narrow gauge Vale of Rheidol section. He was proud of this, as he had spent all his holidays from about 1890 onwards at Aberystwyth, his favourite resort, and had seen the Vale of Rheidol Railway under construction at the turn of the century.

My father had also been a chargeman in the body shop, and my brother had, naturally, also been apprenticed to the trade. Hence when I first said that I wanted to work on engines, and had no interest in spending my life building carriages, the whole family tried to dissuade me. I was told how clean it was working in the carriage shops compared to the loco shops, from where you usually arrived home looking little different from the piece of dirty oil waste hanging from the pocket of your overalls. However engines were in my blood and I could not get enthusiastic about carriages; as far as I was concerned they were merely for people to sit in and be carried about in, whereas a steam engine was a glorious living thing with which nothing really compared. Hence I stuck to my guns and the family reluctantly gave way. The rule in those days was that the first son of a tradesman could be apprenticed free of charge, but the second and subsequent sons had to be paid for, £100 for the five year apprenticeship. The wages in the first two years were barely sufficient to cover this and whilst I cannot now remember what they were before stoppages, for the first year I took home 12/8d per week out of which about ⅞d had to be saved to pay to the company. This left my Mother with the princely sum of five shillings towards feeding and clothing me. Moreover I worked a 47 hour week for that five shillings.

But what a pleasant way to earn money, however little. I was now with engines – not admiring them from afar – and I was working in the premier railway works in the world. On my first day I was allocated Swindon Works Time Check No. 1, which was one of the few allocated to premium apprentices as a temporary measure until the company was satisfied you would make the grade. I was taken to the foreman's office in the B Shed which, like most G.W.R. railway workshop offices, was up steps, so that the foreman had a good view over all his domain. The first things that caught my eye were two nameplates mounted on the wall behind his desk. These were *Isis* and *Stour*, removed from the old River class 2–4–0s when they were taken out of traffic in 1918. Incidentally these plates were still in this same office well after the War but disappeared, I believe, in a shop reorganisation in the early 1960s.

After a few kindly words from Foreman Bullock, I was taken down to the shop floor and over to Chargeman Arthur Dingley's desk. He talked to me for a short while, told me the name of the fitter I was to work with, and then showed me a printed form clipped to a backboard hung by his desk. It was the repair schedule for 0–6–0 Dean Goods 2349, and showed how the repair was planned from the minute it entered factory until it left. It started with a date for stripping the motion, wheels out, boiler out, etc. listed dates all components had to be in the Boiler, Wheel, Machine Shops etc., the date of their return, erecting dates, valve setting and painting dates, etc., etc., ending up with the date the engine was to take its post-repair trial run. Such planning as this is thought to be a very recent introduction but planned progress repairs were certainly in being at Swindon in 1933 and, I will wager, for very many years before that date.

The trial date was given as 28 August 1933 and the date I started work was 31 July. Arthur took me along to the 'engine', called the fitter and that was that. Minutes later I sat on the wooden pit board between the bare frames of 2349 and two things crossed my mind.

The first was 'fancy them paying me for being here in the middle of an engine repair shop', and the second was that there did not seem much chance to me of them getting this engine completed by 28 August. The frame was barer than the proverbial Mother Hubbard's cupboard; no boiler, no wheels or motion, just the frames and the cross members mounted on wooden supports. No overtime was worked in those days, and when I thought of the amount of work that obviously had to be done, I could not visualise this Dean Goods steaming on trials on 28 August. However, a few days later the components started coming back from the various repair shops and, sure enough, on the afternoon of Friday 25 August No. 2349 left B Shed on the traverser table, and Arthur told me I could go on trial on her on the Monday morning.

The thought of this, my first official footplate ride, kept me at a high pitch of excitement over the week-end. I wondered where we would go on the Monday. Surely a tender engine would go at least to Wootton Bassett after a General Repair? However, it was not to be, probably there were more important engines going on trial that day, for the trial inspector decided that up and down the half mile outside the workshops would do. With five on the footplate – the driver and fireman, trial inspector, fitter and myself – I had to keep out of the way as far as possible, standing in the corner peering out of the spectacle plate on the fireman's side. Nothing out of the ordinary was wrong with 2349, and it was back to work in the afternoon.

Obviously, apprentices were generally broken in gently, and for the first week or so the usual tricks were played on them, like being sent to the Tool Stores for a left handed spanner or a rubber hammer. Another initiation trick was painting the back of the heels of the victim's boots with red lead, whilst he stood with his back to one of the engine pits, someone having conveniently gone down into the pit with a small tin of red lead and a brush for the purpose. Not a word would be said to the new apprentice until he was leaving work, when he would be the subject of catcalls and much merriment from the workers of other shops as they left the works en masse.

On the serious side, one of the first things you were taught was the use of a hammer and chisel, a painful experience but one which gave you confidence for the rest of your life when using a hammer. With a heavy hand hammer and a roughing chisel, you were told to rough up the steel footsteps below a loco cab. With the amount of oil in use, these steps could be very slippery and dangerous if not roughed up. As a beginner you might hit the head of the chisel nine times out of ten, but the tenth usually hit the hand gripping the chisel. After a while a bruise would appear and get progressively larger until the chisel was almost obstructed from view – and you were in fact getting roughed up more than the footsteps. . . . After deliberately leaving you alone for a while, the fitter would come and see what sort of mess you were getting into. He would produce a stick of yellow chalk from his overall pocket, carefully chalk the head of the chisel and say, 'That's where you are supposed to hit, lad, not your blooming hand.' So, within a few hours you had learned for life the correct way to use a hammer and chisel, and you knew what the old sages meant when they said one had to be cruel to be kind.

Soon afterwards I was in trial again and this time, on 18 September, it was on a class of engine I never dreamed of riding on – an old Barnum 2–4–0, No. 3217. The Barnums were lovely old engines and even in 1933 seemed to be relics of a by-gone age. They had slotted double frames with outside cranks, a huge dome on the boiler and a tall tapered chimney plus a small cab perched at the back, on the sides of which the individual figures making up the engine number were rivetted in a semi-circle. No. 3217 had not had a heavy repair so was not re-painted, just cleaned down with paraffin rags. Even so, when the fitter and I reported to the Weighbridge House and clambered aboard 3217, I was in seventh heaven, and when the trial inspector decided we would go to Brinkworth, on the South Wales direct line, my delight increased. Tender-first we soon crossed the sidings and main lines to settle on the down relief at the front of one of the timber sheds near Rodbourne Lane signalbox (my old Boards site). Here, after reversing, we waited the signal for the main line. One down train passed and soon afterwards we were given the road, ambling down towards Rushey Platt Junction. Then the driver opened out and we sped westwards with the crank flying and trails of white smoke dying out behind us in the autumn sunshine. Speed was reduced for crossing over to the South Wales line at Wootton Bassett, but in no time we were at Brinkworth. There we were put into the cattle pen siding, where we stayed a considerable time whilst the inspector and fitter went round checking for any signs of overheated bearings, then checking in the smokebox, and also for leaking water or steam joints.

Before returning to Swindon, the inspector stressed upon me the importance of never standing with one foot at the front of the tender and the other on the flap plate. That was the last I saw of him or the fitter until we got back to the works yard. They went around to the front and stood on the footplating in front of the smokebox door, and I soon knew why. Running tender-first was an experience new to me at speed on the main line. Whilst we in the cab were getting the full benefit of the wind and draught, with coal dust flying all around the cab, the experienced pair were standing quite comfortably holding the front handrail, protected by the boiler from the rush of wind created by the speed of the engine. Apparently it was quite usual for the inspector and fitter to return from trial that way, but the apprentice was never allowed round there whilst the engine was in motion.

I soon found out that the warning about the flap plate was very timely, as when we swung over to the up relief immediately after passing Rushey Platt Junction, the tender swung round a split second before the engine and in that instant the flap plate slid over the tender plating. After I had left Swindon, I heard that in 1941 an apprentice was thrown out and killed instantly, passing over the points here, and thereafter apprentices were not allowed on trial runs after this tragic mishap.

The Swindon fitters' apprenticeship involved only a few weeks, or months, on any particular job and then being moved on to other work. Hence my spell in the B Shed soon came to an end, and I passed into the adjacent R Shop to learn the art of lathe work. To start off, to get used to machines, I was put on Joe Mile's nut scragging gang, where the main job seemed to be to feed nuts on to a tap to clean up the threads. Quite a number of nuts stuck and turned on the tap, often tearing the skin on your fingers in the process. It was all in a day's work, and you soon progressed to skilled work, appreciating the accuracy of the machining operations carried out during the repair of components for G.W. locomotives.

Early in 1934 I was transferred to a small machine section sited at the back of the Boiler Shop Stores, popularly known as the Monkey House. This consisted of a narrow shop with a central gangway and a row of automatic machines that produced steel boiler stays on each side. It had a high wire fence on the Stores side and at each end; no doubt that was where the name originated. There was only one entrance, and immediately inside stood the chargeman's desk at which was seated the redoubtable Charlie Shadwell. Apart from Charlie, there were about four or five apprentices and one labourer. I well remember the latter; he was a cheery soul who had transferred from Penrhiwceiler during the depression, and made sure I learned to spell the name of his birthplace even though, at this time the Welsh valleys seemed as far away as Penzance or John o'Groats, and pronouncing Welsh names seemed a way of causing your tongue an injury.

We apprentices fed the steel bars into the automatic, checked a sample of stays as they were made and adjusted the machines as necessary. However the cage was never a popular place, for it was a case of once in there was no escape until the allotted time was over. At 8.00 a.m. Charlie was already there glancing at his morning paper, a minute or two later he bent down to take off his outdoor shoes and put on his working boots. That was the signal for work to start and the machines were started up. Heaven knows when that unwritten rule started, but doubtless it had seen many years before I was put in the cage. Charlie's change of footwear was the controlling factor of work in the Monkey House, not the celebrated hooter. There was no-one who would dare to shut off his machines until Charlie again bent down to change back into his walking shoes about 12.25. The same procedure happened in the afternoon, shoes off 1.35 and back on 5.25, day in and day out. . . .

One Thursday morning whilst working there I felt very sick, and after a while Charlie sent me home. On the Friday I still felt bad, but it was not until Saturday morning that my parents decided that the doctor should be called. He came about 11.00 a.m. and to him I certainly owe my life, for after a brief examination he took me straight to the G.W.R. hospital. By noon I had been operated on for peritonitis, my appendix having burst that morning. I spent the following seven weeks in hospital, and a further similar period convalescing, hence by the time I returned to work I had been transferred from the Monkey House to the A.M. Shop.

During my spell in the A Shop I became a little bolder as, although apprentices were discouraged from leaving their own workshop during working hours, little was said if they had a wander around during the lunch hour. Thereafter, I made regular visits to the two lines of engines awaiting repair outside the shop, and could walk amongst them – much better than the long distance view that I had from The Boards a few years earlier. Whilst the A Shop pilot was still usually an old standard 0–6–0–PT, I was surprised when, in 1934, one of the 0–6 2 pannier tanks that had been rebuilt at Caerphilly from old Rhymney Railway saddle tanks of 1925/6 memory, No. 139, took over for two or three months. As rebuilt, they looked very impressive. Other non-standard shunters that worked as A Shop pilots in the 1930s were No. 807 in 1932, formerly a Barry Railway 0–6–0ST rebuilt as a pannier tank, whilst in 1937 there was No. 671, still a saddle tank, with heavy outside slotted frames, which had come from the Alexandra Docks at Newport.

I also spent the occasional lunch hour on a visit to the Dump, and on one of these in the autumn of 1935, there was my favourite engine, 4–4–0 3398 *Montreal*. During the days when I had 'collected' names, *Montreal* was the rarest of all to see at Swindon, and long after it had been the only named standard engine I had not seen, I was fortunate to catch a glimpse of it standing in Taunton station from a 1928 Trip train. It then still had the old flat brass beading around the splashers, which it retained when sent to Swindon from the West of England for General Repair early in 1930 – easily the last engine of its class to retain that attractive form of embellishment. On release from factory, (having lost the beading) it was shedded for a while at Westbury and worked into Swindon regularly, but soon returned to the West, where 3398 had spent practically all its working life. After seeing it on the Dump for scrapping. I could not resist purchasing one of the name and number plates, which then cost £1 and 7s6d respectively; I wish I still had them now.

Two other Bulldogs which had been pretty scarce at Swindon soon followed *Montreal* to the scrap yard, 3327 *Marco Polo* and 3352 *Pendragon*, both these being Ringers.

Sometime during my apprenticeship, I was amazed to see some Glasgow & South Western Railway 0–6–2Ts in the B Shed. I believe there were three of them, and the numbers 16904, 16908 and 16910 stick in my mind. They were inside the main line end of the shop, and carried no distinguishing marking at all, but beneath the coating of paint the old engine numbers could clearly be made out. I understood they had been sold to one of the big civil engineering contractors, possibly McAlpine, and had come into the B Shed for minor attention. They only stayed a few days and, unfortunately, as I made no record of the event I am not certain of the date, or whether it was three, or only two, engines involved. Nevertheless it was a most unusual and unexpected sight at Swindon.

Some time in 1935 I was transferred to the Brass Shop, where all the brass engine fittings were overhauled. My chief recollection of this smaller shop was of the man who sat there making nameplates. Sitting in his chair, with a large bench before him, he had by his side a massive box full of individual cast letters. The large steel arc plates were already cut to shape and on these he arranged the letters of the selected name. When he was satisfied with the spacing, and not until then, he marked off, drilled and then rivetted the letters on. After fixing on the tubular brass beading surround, the plate was ready for the painter and polisher. He told me, somewhat sadly, that the cast letters then in use, also for all the modern named engines, were hollow whereas for the earlier engines the letters had been solid. Whilst

I was working there, he had to make new nameplates for the two so-called streamline engines, 5005 *Manorbier Castle* and 6014 *King Henry VII*. The old curved plates were replaced by the straight type, and he had to punch out the rivets, retrieve the letters from the old plates, and re-arrange them on the new straight plate ready for rivetting on in the usual way.

Late in 1936 or early in 1937 I was posted back to the B Shed. During the rounds I had learned the fitting and turning part of my apprenticeship, and was now expected to be a useful member of an erecting gang, and not the green innocent I had been when I had started in the same shop in July 1933. Foreman Bullock and his nameplates were still in the office, but this time I was put on Jack Maisey's gang, the chargeman who covered the first few pits from the main line. This was the plum job; Jack's fame at being able to earn piecework money well in advance of the other chargemen was well known. Unlike the other chargemen who usually put a fitter, a mate and an apprentice on one engine, Jack believed in getting components to the various shops as soon as possible after the engine came into shop. Hence directly one was ready over the pit, Jack put a number of his gang on stripping it down, and the speed this was done was unbelievable. Within 24 hours, the engine was picked as clean as a chicken, the boiler, wheels, motion axle boxes etc. being away into the respective repair shops, leaving the men to get back to their 'own' engines. By this method Jack's balance, as the fortnightly piecework payments were known, averaged about 70 per cent compared with about half this on the other gangs, for whom 40 per cent was considered good.

At the time I was on Maisey's gang (as it was generally called), the Bulldog/Duke conversions were underway, and I think his gang did them all; certainly I never saw one done by anyone else. The one I worked on was 3208 *Earl Bathurst*, which theoretically comprised the frame of Bulldog 3403 *Trinidad* and the boiler of Duke 3285 *Katerfelto*. These two had been put into shop together, and stripped (in the Maisey manner) side by side. The two boilers were taken out and away, and the frame (also I believe the wheels) of the Duke taken back out of shop and pushed down the Dump for scrapping. We were left with the bare frames of 3403 which was reassembled with a new Duke type boiler, although quite a number of small components from 3285 were used in the rebuild. I went trial to Brinkworth on 3208 on 4 February 1937, and this proved to be my only trial run during my brief second spell in the B. Shed.

After 3208 had gone into traffic, my fitter and I were put to work on another of the class, intended to be 3210. We had stripped the two engines concerned, 3415 *George A. Wills* and 3281 *Cotswold*, and the components were marked 3210, as was chalked on the cabside. I was aware that the Barnum numbered 3210 was still in service and presumed this old 2-4-0 would be withdrawn before the new 3210 was due in traffic. This did not happen and, at the last moment, the engine was numbered 3211. Almost as soon as it left the shop, the Barnum was taken out of service, but the number was not changed back, and the next rebuild took the number 3210. I never trialled with either, as I was moved to the AE Shop just before 3211 left shops. The B Shed had been a great place to work, steeped in history; parts of it dated back to the start of the factory in 1842, and all the famous broad gauge engines had been repaired there. In 1937, whilst it still mainly dealt with tank engines of the 0-6-0 and 0-4-2 wheel arrangements, tender engines up to the Bulldog class were also repaired there, and I remember 3335 (formerly *Tregothnan*) coming in with a cracked frame, one of the other gangs fitting it with heavy patches.

It was about this time that I became a temporary works guide. There were still large parties from schools visiting Swindon Works, comprising hundreds of children along with their teachers, and the watchmen had no hope of coping with these numbers. The senior apprentices were asked if they would volunteer as guides, and most of us did. One afternoon the volunteers were taken around the pre-scribed route by the chief guide, instructed as to what usually most interested the visitors, also the type of questions most frequently asked. This tour was somewhat similar to the standard one except that it included the carriage shops on the south (or town) side of the main line, which none of us apprentices had been in before. To do this, the parties entered the works at Sheppard Street, which was only about half way from the station to the Tunnel Entrance. To compensate for the extra time in the carriage shops, the B Shed and R Shop of the Loco Works were omitted from the tour.

We used to enjoy these mass visits, as we were allowed home at 12 noon, and after getting cleaned up and changed, we would report back to the Sheppard Street entrance about 1.45. When the visitors arrived, the chief guide would allocate us a party of about 15 to 20 children plus a teacher and off we went, crossing our fingers that we would not be asked any awkward questions. Naturally with children there were such questions, such as, 'What is the weight of that wheel, mister?' or 'How many feet of wood goes into the making of that carriage?' and so on. An inspired quick estimate usually satisfied the questioners, as they had nothing definite to go on either! Still it

No.2971 'Albion' standing in the A Shop reception sidings awaiting Factory attention, 1928.　　　[Author's Collection]

*Engines under repair in the AE Shop, 18 March 1925. Note the traverser table road in the foreground. The engines visible are 4022 'King William' (on the overhead crane), 2–8–0T 4221, 4–6–0 No.2909 'Lady of Provence' and (far right) 2900 'William Dean'.*

[British Railways]

was fun, and as we took leave of the party on their way back to the station, the teacher would usually press a shilling or even a florin into our hands. In those days this seemed a lot of extra money to us.

Another thing we apprentices enjoyed was the annual excursion arranged by the Social and Educational Union to a musical evening at the Albert Hall, in London. Not that we were all that keen on serious music but it was an evening out in Town. We were allowed paid leave for the afternoon and given a combined rail/concert ticket. On arrival at Paddington, we made our own way to the Albert Hall where we had our ticket endorsed, or part removed, or whatever they did. We were soon somewhere up in the dome and sat quietly awaiting the concert. After a couple of minutes the lads would begin leaving one by one, ostensibly to go to the toilet, but in reality down the staircases and outside. We then had an evening amid the bright lights of London, returning to Paddington late in the evening for the train home. Despite the empty seats in the Hall we never heard more about it, although for a few days afterwards we were always apprehensively expecting a call to the Foreman's office 'to explain'.

I was now in the last eighteen months or so of my apprenticeship, which would all be spent (or so I thought) in the AE Shop working mainly on the larger engines. The routine was to start in the middle traverser section where light repairs were carried out, then to prog-ress to the west traverser area where larger engines under-went heavy repairs, and complete the apprenticeship on new construction, a small section of about eight pits sited towards the north-west cor-ner of that area.

Hence I was now working in the holy of holies, as far as a G.W.R. enthusiast was concerned, surrounded by the pride of the locomotive fleet in various stages of dismantling or re-erection. Here I was in the leading locomotive repair and construction workshop in the world, and one that I had gazed on longingly ten years earlier when I saw *King George V* emerge into the sunlight for the very first time.

I was put on Norman McLeod's gang in the centre bay, dealing with Light Repairs. The chances were that I would get trial trips more frequently than when working on heavy repair work. On light repairs, boilers did not have to be taken out of the frames, most of the work being connected with axleboxes, cylinders, reversing gear, rods and motion, the components that were subject to heavy wear. Cleaning down was kept to a minimum, so it was a fairly dirty job, but 'plenty of grime, plenty of trials' was my motto.

I was on McLeod's gang for about three months during which time I went out on trial five times, on each occasion to Wootton

Bassett, as was customary for tender engines after light repair. These trials were –

| | | |
|---|---|---|
| 7 June 1937 | 4041 | *Prince of Wales* |
| 30 June 1937 | 4016 | *Knight of the Golden Fleece* |
| 6 July 1937 | 2944 | *Highnam Court* |
| 20 August 1937 | 2927 | *Saint Patrick* |
| 3 September 1937 | 2608 | (Aberdare class) |

It was not until 1937 that I first worked in Swindon shed. I had not even been there before as it was sited in a most inaccessible place for the railway enthusiast, not visible from any public place apart from a train going around the Gloucester line. It could only be reached by continuing through a second longish tunnel directly following the main tunnel entrance to the works. From the end of this second tunnel, the shed was still some distance northwards, reached across numerous sidings. Thus it was never included in normal works visits, and visitors were only taken there by special arrangements beforehand.

Occasionally one of us would be sent there from the A Shop to attend to some minor fault which required specialist tools, or if an engine ex-factory developed a fault which did not warrant it being returned to the workshop. The fitter and I were sent there one day, carrying a heavy bag of tools. It was a long walk to the shed, although naturally it was full of interest to me. There was the old straight shed where the centre five of the nine roads converged on to a turntable area at the far end. There was a lead from that turntable to another table in the second part of the shed, a standard round-house, alongside. Normally the larger tender engines were stabled in the roundhouse with shunting and other smaller ones in the straight shed. Obviously, as would be expected, there were always exceptions to this rule.

Not far from the straight shed and closer to the Gloucester line was the Stock Shed where, in my day, a few engines were stabled when not immediately required for traffic. One or two engines shedded at Swindon but waiting factory were also located there. I particularly remember 0–4–2T No. 1477 out of the dozen or so engines that were there all told. A few years earlier this large six-road straight shed had housed a considerable number of engines stored due to the depression of the early to mid-1930s, so many being sent there that they filled the sidings outside as well. These mainly consisted of some fifteen 0–6–2Ts of the 6700 class and a number of new 5275 series 2–8–0Ts which were converted to 2–8–2Ts before they had even been put into traffic, along with a few constituent

0–6–2Ts temporarily out of work, plus some redundant steam car engines. The shed itself had about 75 to 80 engines allocated there, but of course that number was always supplemented by others of all classes ex-factory that were 'run in' before returning to their home sheds.

Before leaving the light repair section of the A Shop there are three other things I recall while working there. The first was the job we had one day re-wheeling an R.O.D. 2–8–0. With its wheels in position on the pit road, the engine itself was suspended from the overhead gantry. Gradually it was lowered so that the axle boxes we were guiding would slide home gently into the horns in the frame. Each time one or other box would not go in and immediately rotated on the journal when touched by the horn; up the engine would have to go again for another try. After going up and down in this fashion for what seemed like ages to all concerned, all was well, and eight sighs of relief were heard – until drowned by the gantry driver yelling down to us, 'And about bloody time too!'

The second recollection was when we had to check and spruce up two 4–4–0s of the Earl class, which had just had their nameplates removed at the time. These were required for a Royal Train due to run on the Cambrian section, and the pair of them were examined, cleaned and tested to perfection. That was the only time during my apprenticeship that I worked overtime, and that only for about one and a half hours.

My third memory was the stripping for scrap of one of the early 4300 class 2–6–0s, 4306, whose withdrawal was booked against the building of one of the 4–6–0 Granges. In fact some components were used in the new engines, and I recollect when 6800 *Arlington Grange* was under construction that a number of parts were stamped 4313, crossed out and restamped 6800. (The withdrawal of 4313 had been booked against the construction of 6800). The fitter and I stripped 4306 down in just one week, at least the engine parts, and as it was a very dirty job we earned 'dirt money', as it was called, the only time I ever had any despite countless other equally dirty jobs.

In September 1937 I moved down to the main west bay where the heavy repairs and new work was carried out. For standard scheduled heavy repairs, a new system had been introduced about three or four years earlier. There were four sections, the first dealing with stripping and despatching the components to the repair shops; the second with frame repairs, axle box horns etc; the third with re-assembly; and the fourth with finishing off. Apprentices normally skipped the stripping section, spent a period on either of the next two and then moved on to the fourth. There were also one or two other gangs that dealt with out-of-course or intermediate repairs and, after a short spell on the frame section, I had a few weeks on one of those. There I went trial three times in rapid succession –

16 December 1937   5916   *Trinity Hall*   To Dauntsey Incline
19 December 1937   4906   *Broughton Hall*   To Dauntsey Incline
6 January 1938      6002   *King William IV*   To Dauntsey station

So by early 1938 I had footplated a King in the course of my duties. Although any footplate ride was still a major thrill, a run on one of these was the last word.

A week or so later I moved on to Section D, the finishing-off group in the progress repair system. It was there that you might notice wisps of smoke curling up from the chimneys of engines whose boiler tubes had not seen smoke for some three or four weeks. There was a 'No Smoking' rule throughout the factory; in other shops men would go out to the toilets and have a puff, but you were timed there and if you exceeded either ten minutes, or two visits in one day, you were called to the Foreman's office 'to explain'. Hence one or two would get in a smokebox and close the door for a quick puff, leaving only the tell-tale faint trails of smoke emerging from the chimney. Although quite obvious, a blind eye was turned to such practices even by the foreman, the chargeman ensuring that the occasional cigarette did not interfere with work.

The same happened when we had an unofficial mid-morning break. It was the unwritten law to get down in the pit under the engine to eat your sandwiches then. Although one of the foremen often walked around the shop and knew perfectly well what was going on, nothing was said provided you kept – more or less – out of his direct sight, and stayed in the pit for your snack.

Working on Section D gave ample opportunity to go trial. Sometimes an apprentice was not keen to go, and the chargeman would call for a 'volunteer'. He need not look any further; there was one lad always ready and eager! In the two months or so I was on the section, I went trial on six further occasions –

26 January 1938    6308                        To Wootton Bassett
1 February 1938    4566                        To Wootton Bassett
15 February 1938   4969   *Shrugborough Hall*   To Dauntsey station
17 February 1938   5564                        To Wootton Bassett
21 March 1938      6018   *King Henry VI*      To Brinkworth
25 March 1938      5012   *Berry Pomeroy Castle*   To Dauntsey Incline

Of the trial runs it was the one on 5564, for which I had volunteered, that I recall best. When we were approaching Bassett on the down run, the Inspector's nose suddenly rose, sniffing the air. Before the rest of us, he had detected the hot fishy smell that denoted a hot axle box. As we were so close to the station, he allowed us to continue after slowing up to walking pace, and had us put into a siding. There we stayed a long time letting the box cool and soaking it with oil. Eventually we returned to Swindon at a crawl, the fitter dropping down here and there to apply further liberal applications of oil.

The run on the King (6018) was exceedingly pleasant. It was a nice bright afternoon and, just before we left the Weighbridge House, the popular Assistant Shop Foreman, Wally Dew, joined us on the footplate. Although I did not know it then, whenever Wally accompanied trial runs the chances were that the destination was Brinkworth. On arrival we stabled 6018 in the cattle pen siding, as was usual, and off went Wally up the slope to the village. It was then I was told he had relatives there, and we would be staying until he returned – hardly a hardship, on a beautiful afternoon, on the footplate of a King whose trial had produced no problems. It was late in the afternoon before we saw our Assistant Shop Foreman again, and this was followed by a brisk run back to the factory and the stabling of the engine on one of the roads of the works turntable to end a very memorable afternoon.

The one on *Berry Pomeroy Castle* proved to be my last trial run; I could hardly complain, having had seventeen, including a Barnum and two Kings. I never worked on new construction, as a few days later I was called for interview in the Drawing Office, almost under Brunel's drawing board that used to hang above the swing doors into the office. There I was offered the chance to complete my apprenticeship in the small drawing office at Newport Docks. Despite my regret at leaving my home town and going off into the unknown, I knew there was only one answer.

I was transferred on 11 April to the Test House, a transition stage between the noise, dirt, hustle and bustle of the workshops and the quiet cleanliness of a small office. The Test House was the ideal transition place, a kind of workshop, but spotlessly clean, where peace and solitude reigned amidst the testing machines and chains to be tested.

On 25 April I started work at Newport, my days at Swindon over for, as it turned out, I never returned there either to work or reside. It had been a very happy place for me, both as a keen young enthusiast in my school days and later as an apprentice at the works.

Much of the Swindon I knew has now gone, but when I pay a visit or pass through by train, there are still many familiar places to recall those days half a century ago. The Boards are still there, even if not the original fence, and the former Barnes' yard is still full of timber although the logs and traction engines are long since gone. The old Dump area still remains, although sidings Nos. 1 to 18 were picked up about 1977 and shrubs now grow in their place. The A Shop, Barn, turntable area and B Shed all survive despite having new identities and being used for different purposes these days. The C.M. & E.E.'s offices with the broad gauge engines carved into the stonework are still there, although the station is now hardly recognisable. The down side has gone and on the up side the old Up main (No. 5) platform is now the down main, and the old Up Gloucester (No. 8, the Cheltenham Flyer platform) is now the up main. The subway entrance to the station is cleaner and smarter these days, and the works Tunnel Entrance survives, as does St. Marks Church, the Mechanics Institute plus the Medical Fund Health Centre – the latter now part of the N.H.S., of course.

I knew it all as it used to be and, although I preferred it that way, progress goes on. Doubtless the youngsters there today will, in years to come, treasure Swindon as at present I do the Swindon past. I am glad I was born there, especially during the height of Great Western supremacy; I would not like to have missed what was a wonderful experience.

## ACKNOWLEDGEMENTS

*It is my pleasant duty to thank the following for their help during the compilation of these reminiscences. Firstly my wife whose patience and encouragement ensured rapid progress; secondly the staff at Swindon Reference Library who were always most helpful. I would also like to thank friends who helped with photographs or in other ways – Ray Bowen, Brian Harry, Stephen Jones, Dr. Stuart Owen Jones, R. C. Riley; also British Rail, H. C. Casserley and Lens of Sutton for allowing me to reproduce the photographs credited to them, and to John Reed for allowing me to use one of the photographs taken by his late grandfather. I am also grateful to one or two other unknown photographers whose efforts, I regret to say, can only be acknowledged to the author's collection.*

*Eric R. Mountford*